25 YEARS OF SANTA STORIES

Kids Say the

DARNDEST THINGS

to Santa Claus

DON KENNEDY

VOLUME 3

First Edition Published 2022 – Copyright Registration Donald Kennedy
Library of Congress Control Number: 2020914778
USA – BookBaby: Pennsauken, New Jersey
Print ISBN: 978-1-66785-613-1
eBook ISBN: 978-1-66785-614-8

Contents

"Santa Claus has the right idea,
visit people only once a year."

Victor Borge
Danish American Comedian, Conductor and Pianist
1909-2000 Born in Copenhagen, Denmark

CHAPTER 1

25 Years of Santa Stories: Santa Tells All!

Ever wonder what children and Santa Claus talk about each Holiday season? Have you wondered what it is like to don the Santa suit and portray jolly old Saint Nick? Or, what happens when a little one has an "accident" while on Santa's knee? Hopefully, this book can help answer those and other questions. For the past 25 years, (actually, 2022 is year 29, but who is counting...), I have volunteered as Santa Claus for charities and organizations that did not have the funds to hire a Santa. This included Boys & Girls Clubs, children's hospitals, military bases, National Guard recreation halls, police, fire and sheriff's department halls, women's & children's centers, schools, churches, children's centers, temporary housing, community centers, resorts, apartments, and everything in between. The last few years, I have been Santa for the children and grandchildren of close family friends as well. That was very special for all of us and a unique experience as well. Just imagine Santa finally trying to leave a home, I had not totally thought that through, for sure!

1

I got my start portraying Santa Claus when a good friend of mine got ill the night before a large Boys & Girls Club holiday party appearance. He had volunteered as Santa for many years and had talked me into being his Head elf for that particular event. When he could not go, he suggested that I fill in for him. I did and as they say, the rest is history. That full story is included in this book.

I do not know of anyone who just woke up one day and declared (to themselves) that, "I'm Santa Claus!" Fortunately, some of us actually do decide to fill that role for their communities and beyond. I am not exactly sure if there is a Santa University or advanced degree. Volunteer Santa's are not to be found every-where, so when you make that commitment, you need to stick with it. Most charities and organizations want you back year after year plus the word spreads. In communities, large and small, there is a great need out there. Volunteer Santa's hear about each other and often end up filling in as needed during illness, work, and family obligations. You cross paths and become friends. It is a very small network and I have met some of the very best of humanity.

I want to do a special shout out or tip of Santa's cap to all the wonderful, amazing, talented, and selfless elves and Mrs. Claus' at all of the locations who give of their time and talents to organize and staff events to help make memories for kids every Holiday season. I have always truly enjoyed watching these fellow volun-teers' reactions to the unfiltered, blunt, honest, humorous, and heartfelt comments from all the precocious "little characters" we encounter. It is not something you ever forget, nor does it ever get old. Out of the mouth of babes as the saying goes. It is not easy to be an elf. You must have a good demeanor, be patient, organized, (imagine keeping 50 to 100 children ages 3 to 8 in a line), plus keep your emotions somewhat in check. Often Santa's helpers know the children, including their own, who visit Santa. Pretty special times for them all.

I have enjoyed sharing these moments with countless elves and Mrs. Claus' including members of all the military services, first responders, teachers, church leaders, nurses, doctors, social workers, and from so many more professions. I know they get as much or more than even I do during this very special time of the year. In particular, I want to recognize elves Lois "Joei" Wood, Ron Sakaniwa, Joel A. Leong, Niki Gratson-Middleton, Jonathan "JT" Smith, Martin Deaver, James Boggs, Karina Durante, Larry Elliott, John Simonton, Bill Montague, Andrew Clark, Jane Finstrom, Gray Schmidt, Bonzai, Susana Poulin and Joseph Fry. Plus Mrs. Claus' Teresa Lusk and Marlena Kesler. Again, Santa's cap off to all of them.

There is something about being at a Santa's appearance for several hours with the same children, their parents, and grandparents that is different than a shopping mall setting. Now, do not get me wrong, we need these Santa appearances just as much due to the volume of children who need to be seen and heard each year. Many of these Santa's are friends of mine and do an excellent job. However, it is a different situation. There it is a very limited time, a quick hello, your name and age, your Christmas wishes, smile (hopefully) for a picture and done. I never totally realized for a long time that other than seeing Santa on TV, in videos, in books and the like, children do not get real quality time with jolly old St. Nick. At Santa appearances for charitable and community organizations, however, most run anywhere from two to four hours, which gives children a longer time to be around and visit with Santa. It also gives kids who may be too timid initially to meet Santa a chance to observe things and build up their courage to find their "Santa legs." I can always tell the little ones who are standing back, are shy, the first timers, etc. I often encourage parents and grandparents not to force the kids to meet Santa, especially right away. Since there is often several hours at such events, I encourage them to let their kids warm up to the idea rather than push them into it. I know everyone wants their kids to be part of the whole tradition but give them some space. Imagine a little child, especially for the first time, looking at this icon with long white hair and beard, full plush red suit, boots, etc. with the ability to grant wishes, deliver presents and create miracles. Why would a child just rush up and meet him, especially after their parents and grandparents have told them over and over not to talk to strangers! All in good time is my advice.

This book is the third of three that I have written. The first came out in the fall of 2019, the second in the late fall, early January of 2020/2021. All have the same title, just a volume # change each time. I never intended to write these books at all. It started out as an annual posting on my personal Facebook page of my Top 10 Humorous and Top 10 Heartwarming stories after each Santa season for five years. I kept getting comments from friends and family saying the same thing, "you need to write a book." A good friend and former colleague wrote, "Don, there's a book here." So, I stopped making excuses and did it. Wow, what an adventure that was, and continues to be! After the first book was published, I received such an outpouring of positive comments that I decided to keep sharing. Book 4, the final one, will be a combining of all three previous books plus lots more photos and illustrations into a larger size, hard cover book, kind of a coffee table book. Stay tuned for when I will be able to pull that project together.

After each Santa appearance, starting with the first one, I wrote down a half dozen or so of my favorite stories that had taken place. Over the years, I wrote down over 2, 000 stories on scraps of paper that I stored in those proverbial shoe boxes. When I decided, (actually, hounded into it) to write the first book, I sifted through everything and produced about 700+ of the best of the best stories. The first book featured about 100 stories, the second 275 and this one has 350 new stories. Since there are three books, I have rewritten and repeated just a few parts of some chapters in each that helps set up new readers, so it all makes sense to them. Otherwise, everything is new in each book. For this book, I also added a look into the first two books to bring new readers up to speed. Also, I did not stop being Santa after the first 25 years, so years 26, 27 and 28 brought more stories included here. Two special notes I'd like to make here. First, I refer to myself in the various stories in all of the books as Santa, I and me. I trust that it isn't too confusing. All three are the same Santa Don rolled into one. Second, is that kids use words such as "cause," "wanna," "gonna," "I's," plus many more that are, of course, not correct English. I kept them as is because that's what they said and who am I to correct the way children speak as they grow up. I tried to highlight all of those, but I'm sure I missed some. Oh, and just imagine the fun I had with spell-check and editor programs constantly trying to change those spellings and grammar!

All three books are available both in paperback and eBook on sites like: Amazon, Barnes & Noble, Google, Apple, BookBaby's Bookshop, Target, Walmart, eBay and many more. You can also follow Santa on my special Facebook page: SantaStoryteller/ DonKennedy. There are several YouTube videos plus an interview/ reading on YouTube with the Hawaii Writer's Guild's "Inside the Writer's Studio," episode twenty-five with Host Eila Algood. Feel free to reach out to me as well at donhkennedy@msn.com.

Just a quick note about the many references to Hawaii in this book. I semi-retired to Oahu Island in late 2019. If I used Hawaiian words in some of the stories, I tried to also mention the meaning in English . The key words, just in case, are keiki, (child) Mele Kalikimaka, (Merry Christmas) Aloha, (greetings, love, farewell) Ohana, (family and extended family) Tutu (grandmother) Papa, (grandfather) Kumu, (teacher) mele, (music) Hale, (home) and Mahalo (thanks). The "shaka" hand sign referred to is the one with the thumb and pinkie finger out and the three middle fingers folded in. It's the universal sign on all the islands of greetings and farewell. Double "shaka" refers to using both hands to display the sign at the same time. Hope this helps.

I deeply and humbly appreciate all the response, encouragement, critique, and advice so far in this journey into the wonderful, magical world of Santa Claus and children.

Again, if you have ever wondered what children say to Santa Claus, you are in the right place. They surely do say the darndest things! This is for every child, (and all those who still are at Christmas), parents, grandparents, family, friends, elves, fellow Santa's, and Santa event organizers everywhere.

Let the Santa stories begin as Santa tells all! Or as they say in the Hawaiian Islands, "Let's talk story!"

CHAPTER 2

The Very First Time - How It All Began

25 years ago, in early December, a close friend of mine had shared with me that he was a volunteer Santa. He made appearances at various holiday parties for charities and organizations that did not have funds to hire a Santa. He had suggested for some time that I should dress up as an elf and join him. I finally stopped making excuses and agreed to join in. The night before my first elf adventure at a major Boys & Girls Club children's party, he came down with a bad virus. He suggested that I go in his place as Santa Claus. Very skeptical at first, as you can imagine, I had a hundred questions. But finally, I agreed, took his Santa duffle bag and off I went. He offered a backup suit, but I declined, what on earth could happen, right?

About one hundred children, ages 4 to 8, were waiting at the center draped with festive holiday décor. A dozen staff volunteers, and several dozen parents were present as well. There were refreshments and small gifts for all the kids. I had stopped on the way and bought several hundred large candy canes to make sure every child received something. The children all had a meal prior to my arrival.

Santa had a head elf and two Santa's helpers. Sitting on a large stuffed chair with a Christmas tree on one side and wrapped gifts on the other, Santa looked on as the children all sang holiday songs for about 15 minutes. Then each of the various age groups performed a skit they had written with their staff members. It was really precious. Santa jumped in a few times to sing and dance along with the children. It was totally impromptu, and the kids loved it. Wow, this is really fun, I thought to myself. Then the announcement was made for the children to line up single-file and approach Santa. The head elf introduced each child to Santa by their first name. I then asked each child their age and had them hold up their fingers to show their age, something I still do to this day. Santa matched each finger with theirs which created a special type of high five.

Santa then asked each child what their wishes were for Christmas, followed by a photo and giving the kids a large candy cane. Each child also received a small gift. So far, so good. I remember thinking that this really is not that hard.

The next child came up, a 6-year-old boy, who replied when I asked what his wishes were, "Well, I wrote you a letter, don't you remember?" Thinking fast, I told him that Mrs. Claus took care of all the letters. OK, that worked. A little boy marched proudly up to Santa when it was his turn and asked, "Mommy says I's impossible, whats that get me?"

A dozen kids later and I had my first "accident" when a very excited little boy "urped" on Santa's leg. That was when I recalled my friend offering me that second suit. Santa needs a backup suit at all appearances for sure! The best I could do in this case was take a short break, clean up the best I could, and go back at it. A tiny bit of panic was starting to creep in.

A few kids later, a little girl came up, stared at Santa, and blurted out, "You better drink skim milk or 2% milk cause you look really fat!" Her mother was horrified but I told her that Mrs. Claus had me on a new diet. She seemed satisfied with that. A boy, 7 years old, came up, folded his arms in front of his chest and declared, "I hope you do better than last year!" Next up was a girl who announced that she was "Going to gets married in couple weeks and has twins." Her dad looked on with amazement since she was just 6. Another little boy was really amusing himself by trying to tell me his favorite joke until he totally forgot the punchline. Another little guy blurted out, "My grandpa says I's a work in process 'n go easy on me." Being puked on aside, this was becoming heartwarmingly fun.

Donning the Santa suit taught me several things, but mainly that you need to be quick on your feet and ready for just about anything. You need to listen carefully and not promise the world. I was also in total wonder at these amazing little characters, how their minds worked and what they had to say. I also learned that what a child hears, they do repeat. That was borne out by a little boy starting to tell Santa what his daddy said in the car on the way to the party about the other drivers. His dad stopped him just in the nick of time!

On went the night, about three hours in all. As I walked through the center to the office to change, about a dozen kids waited at the front door entrance. I wondered what that was all about. Turns out they wanted to see Santa make his exit, plus see the sleigh and all the reindeer. That explained why my Santa friend told me to carefully disappear from the party when all the children had been seen and get changed into your "civies." I left quietly and inconspicuously out to the car. Instead of just driving home, I sat back for a bit and collected myself. For some reason I will never know, I pulled out a pen and a notepad and wrote down about a dozen notes of what the kids had said. On the drive home, I realized that this was one of the most meaningful days of my life. The next day, I returned the Santa suit to my friend, (washed), and told him about my experience. He was most happy that his prediction that I would be a good Santa was correct. And, as they say, the rest is history!

CHAPTER 3

A Grown Up Christmas Wish

As I sit down to finalize writing this on Mother's Day 2022, the invasion and war in Ukraine is in its third month. Writing a book can be a daunting project, especially when you are an amateur like me and have a schedule to meet. You cannot always pick your preferred times and places to write if you are on a strict schedule. In my case, since the three books I have written are considered holiday books, the timeline is pretty much set in order to be published in time for the holiday period.

In this case, however, writing this as war is raging and children are in harm's way, turns out to be a timely opportunity to share a letter I received several years ago from a mom serving in the military. I had gone to a military base in early December to be Santa for a children's event. As always, I had to make a special stop at the visitors/security area to be cleared. Since I carry two duffle bags/suitcases, each with a full Santa suit and all the trimmings, I always get raised eyebrows, a few chuckles, and some good-natured teasing from the security officers before I head on my way to the recreation center. In this case, the officer said,

"I know who you are and where you're going. My kids have a special letter to give you from my wife. They've all been pretty good this year, so go easy on them," he added. I smiled and off I went on my newest Santa mission.

Sure enough, about halfway through the long line of children, a group of three kids came up. Their ages were 3, 5 and 8. After we visited and each told me their Christmas wishes, the oldest child gave me a letter. "This is from our mom, she's in Germany and emailed it to our dad to print it out for you," she said. "She won't be here for Christmas," she added. I told her that I would read the letter as soon as I got back to the North Pole. I also told the three kids that I would stop in Germany on Christmas Eve, find their mom, and give her a big hug from all of them and their dad. That brightened up their faces.

I finished all the visits with the children, changed into my "civies" and got out to my car. As I always do now, I sat back, reflected, and wrote down a dozen or so memories from that afternoon. I also pulled out the special letter. I get dozens and dozens of letters each holiday season. Most of them are from the children with their Christmas wishes, but this one seemed to have a special significance. As I read it, I could not help myself and I really teared up. I always try to keep my emotions in check when portraying Santa, but since I was alone, I let myself feel all the emotions that flooded over me.

Here's moms' letter to Santa:

"Aloha Santa Claus. Mele Kalikimaka! I'm writing this to you from Germany where I'm deployed. By now you've met my family. I am so very blessed with all of them. I won't be with them this Christmas but will do a Facetime as they are unwrapping their presents. It will have to do for this year. As a little girl growing up in Kailua, Hawaii, I treasured our holiday traditions. To get in the mood for Christmas here in Germany, I was scrolling down some holiday songs on YouTube. When I came to this particular one, I listened to four versions sung by Barbra Streisand, Kelly Clarkson, Amy Grant and the original by Natalie Cole. It seemed to say it all for me this year. So, I'm sharing it with you. The title is: My Grown Up Christmas List by David Foster (famed Canadian musician and composer). Here are all the lyrics.

"Do you remember me, I sat upon your knee. I wrote to you my childhood fantasies. Well, I'm all grown up now, but still need you somehow. I'm not a child, but my heart still came dream. So, here's my lifelong wish, my grown-up Christmas list, not for myself, but for a world in need. No more lives torn apart, that wars would never start, and time would heal all hearts. Everyone would have a friend, that right would always win, and love would never end. This is my grown-up Christmas list. As children we believed, the grandest sight to see, was something lovely wrapped beneath the tree. But heaven surely knows that packages and bows, can never heal a hurting human soul. No more lives torn apart, that wars would never start, and time would heal all hearts. Everyone would have a friend, that right would always win, and love would never end, this is my grown-up Christmas list. What is this illusion called the innocence of youth, maybe only in that blind belief can we ever find the truth? No more lives torn apart, that wars would never start, and time would heal all hearts. Everyone would have a friend, that right would always win, and love would never end. This is my grown-up Christmas list, this is my only lifelong wish, this is my grown-up Christmas list."

Please stay safe and healthy Santa in this very difficult time we live in. Many Mahalos for being there for my keiki (kids) and all the keiki you spend time with this Christmas season. I truly hope and pray that you also meet my husband at the front entrance. He'll be on the look-out for you and your "sleigh." If not, please know that he is just as appreciative of your time and service for all of us. As you know, service comes in many forms. Merry, Merry Christmas. Tons and tons of Aloha, Leilani, just another military mom."

CHAPTER 4

Yes Virginia, Santa Really Does Know Hawaiian!

Please bear with me as this story is actually three or four stories in one and longer than usual, but I felt it needed to be added to volume three. It combines Hawaiian Olelo (language) classes, one of my unique nicknames, Santa's role in wildfire recovery periods and a young Hawaiian family who lost everything in a fire on the mainland recently.

Before I moved to Hawaii the end of 2019, I had been a very frequent visitor to the islands for 40 years. I have always had a deep respect and admiration for the Hawaiian and Pacific Islander people, their culture, history, and way of life. I have always been an island boy in spirit, so I felt a natural connection and have been welcomed.

Even though I knew a few key words and phrases, I wanted to learn so much more basic Hawaiian when I came to the islands. I saw on local TV that there was to be a Hawaiian language class offered by the University of Hawaii at Manoa. Reviving and sharing the Hawaiian language are a true blessing. Our Kumu's (teachers) were Paige Okamura and Akea Kahikina. I drove an hour and a half to the university campus, then spent more time searching for a parking space plus locating the classroom. Finally inside, I found over two hundred other people in what was expected to be a class of thirty! It turns out that in that large group of people were several lifetime close friends of mine for over 30 years who lived in Manoa. We did not know each other were in the same room for several days. I am going to use some first names in this story which will make more sense later on. In attendance were Oahu friends Joel (teacher's pet, mentor & my personal professor), Marmie (everyone's Aunty) and special new friend Manono who lives on the big island of Hawaii.

The classes were held weekly on Wednesday afternoon at 3 pm at the UH campus in Manoa and held in person until the pandemic arrived and went virtual thereafter. It was a wonderful experience with the Kumu's being very educational, but lighthearted as well. They mixed it up exactly right. Having my three fellow students was also a blessing. Marmie put the entire program into binders for me and Joel provided a wonderful language program from Kamehameha Schools. Joel also always found time during class to provide me with explanations and homework! I gained a new nickname as well. Early on in class, when asked by our Kumu's in Hawaiian what my name was and where I was from, I replied, "o ko'u inoa' o Makaha, kahi a'u e noho nei Don." The class started laughing and my friends buried their heads in their hands. I had transposed it and replied that I was "Makaha" from "Don." To this day I am still called "Makaha" by friends and neighbors. I guess I will never live that down.

A special bonus I treasured was joining Joel, his wife Lissa, Preston, his wife Tammy, son Eric, daughter Mia, Marmie and Manono for dinner after class. Sometimes other family sons Chase, Spencer, Ryan, and family would also join in. The two families live in Manoa and since class was over about 4:15 pm, the drive back to the Waianae Coast for me to get to Makaha (or Don Valley) on the H1 would have been untimely to say the least! Normally it takes me about an hour and 15 minutes, but during peak periods, much longer. So, the families invited me weekly to stay, have dinner and drive home later in the evening when the traffic was better. Of course, it was also time for my personal tutor Joel to do some after class language drills!

OK, I hope that explains the Hawaiian language part of this story plus my mentioning of various first names. Soon you will also see the many benefits of gaining some basic knowledge and use of this wonderful language as well.

For the past half dozen years, I have portrayed Santa Claus with a Christian family relief/support organization at the site of wild-fires in the Western USA. I made Santa visits at various temporary housing locations in particular in Oregon and California plus several other states. So why would Santa play a part in the aftermath of these tragedies? I wondered that myself when I first got the call about volunteering for this role. The call came from a good friend who lived in Northern California and knew of my Santa volunteer work. Turns out extensive research showed that the adults of the families affected by tragic wildfires have grief counselors, social service workers and temporary housing staff to rely on. Children, especially those twelve and under, not so much. Mickey and Minnie, the Muppets and other children's icons were all considered to be invited to be there for the kids, but it turned out that the #1 choice to provide support to the children was Santa Claus. The reasoning was that Santa brings good cheer, comfort, hope and encouragement all rolled into one. And so, it began.

The longtime friend I mentioned earlier, who serves in the military and was an elf at many of my past Santa appearances, was fighting wildfires and got me involved for the very first time.

Typically, the very worst wildfire season is in the late fall but this year, 2021, it started early. I had just returned from a week of Santa visits. My good friend Marmie gave me a ride to and from Honolulu airport for the flight to the mainland. I told her a little bit of this next story but wanted to fill it all in. It will tie everything together and hopefully make sense of my ramblings up to this point.

At one temporary housing site in Northern California, I met a young Hawaiian family who had just relocated 4 months earlier from Ewa Beach, Oahu, Hawaii. They had lost their apartment in the fire. The family included Mom, Dad, and four sons, Maui (9), Ryan (7), Spencer (5 "and a half" as he pointed out numerous times) and Keahi (3). Everyone had incredibly sad faces, to say the least, when I arrived.

Santa greeted the family with a double "Shaka" sign and "Aloooooha Keiki from Ewa Beach, Mele Kalikimaka early!" The kids' eyes got big and round, their jaws dropped almost in unison, and they came running. They gave me a huge group bearhug with big, bright smiles. Mom started crying and Dad's eyes welled up with tears. Dad was a big, big man.

I asked each child their name, age and what they loved and missed the most about Hawaii. Malasada's, Wet n' Wild, youth sports, school, and neighborhood friends, Ohana (family) beach time and luaus were on the top of the list.

I have found over the years that finding some kind of a special connection to each child at a fire shelter really helps, whatever that happens to be. It helps break the ice and gets everyone to open up. Often it has to do with their names, favorite locations, a song, anything to distract from the pain and sadness of the moment. Sometimes it just happens naturally. Sometimes Santa gets extra special help like the names of the family members of my friends in Manoa.

I asked Maui if he knew he had a famous song written about him. He replied, "No, I do?" I asked if he knew of Israel Kamakawiwo'ole or Izzy or Iz, the beloved island musician. He said, "Yes, he sings about the rainbows." I told him he also sang a hit song called "Maui Hawaiian Sup'pa Man." He got extremely excited and asked to know more. I told him if he and his brothers would play their pretend ukulele's, I would sing the song for him. The three Keiki all strummed along as I sang, "Mischievous, marvelous, magical Maui, Hero of this land. The one, the only, the ultimate Hawaiian Sup'pa Man. Oh, Maui, Maui, Maui, Hawaiian Sup'pa Man!" Maui just beamed. Ryan, Spencer, and Keahi all looked at their older brother and said, "You're famous."

Ryan was the spokesman for the keiki. He said, "Santa, Santa, I got a joke to tell you." I said I loved good jokes. He said, "What did Sushi A say to Sushi B?" I told him I did not know. He replied, "Wasa B?" He laughed and laughed and laughed and everyone in the room joined in. I told him I knew another Ryan in Hawaii (Joel's son) who also had a wonderful family just like theirs and works for Hawaiian Airlines. Ryan said they flew on Hawaiian to come to Northern California. He then got very serious and asked how Santa would find them at Christmas since they did not have a place to live. Santa told them he had special GPS and can find everyone just like he did today at the shelter. Ryan said, "Like Spidey sense, huh?" Maui added, "Wow, superpowers!!!"

Making my way down the line I told Spencer that I knew another Spencer in Hawaii (Preston's son) and he was a great fisherman, waterman, and photographer. I added that he had a twin brother Chase who was also a great fisherman and waterman. Spencer looked up at his mom and said, "Can I get a twin brother Chase too?" His Mom rolled her eyes and replied, "Honey it's a little too late for that." Spencer replied with those two dreaded words for every parent, "But why?" Mom said, "Ask your father."

Little Keahi had finally warmed up to Santa and now wanted to sit on his lap. He looked up at me and said, "I'm littleist." I told him I knew another little boy in Hawaii that was his same age who was getting bigger and taller every day. I also told him the boy's name also started with a K just like his. He looked up and said, "Really, what's it?" "His name is Kupa'a and he's my friend Ryan's son," I said. He smiled big and replied, "He's little like me, huh?" He asked, "Would he play with me?" I told him I was sure that he would. He stroked Santa's beard and rested his head on my chest and fell asleep. His mom told me that he had hardly slept since the fire. I held him sleeping as long as I could. It was awfully hard to finally get up as he was so relaxed and at peace.

We gave each child a gift, some candy and said our goodbyes. The Keiki asked Santa to say Aloha to all their friends and Ohana (family) on the islands. I promised that I would. Mom said "Mahalo Nui Papa." Dad whispered, "I don't know who you are, but my blessings go with you."

Santa finished by saying he would see them all on Christmas Eve, "shoots" (yes, OK, let's do it) and "a hui hou! (See you, till we meet again)" Ryan & Spencer jumped in and replied, "I think Santa knows Hawaiian better than you do Maui." Their older brother said, "Watch it you two, you're gonna end up on the naughty list, like always." With that, Santa made his way to the next shelter.

And now, as the famous commentator Paul Harvey would say, you know the rest of the story... or stories. And yes, Santa Don also knows enough Spanish and Japanese to get by during a visit. The moral of the story is that you can never know too many languages as you will never know when they may come in handy. I think my Kumu's Paige and Akea plus Professor Joel would be proud.

SPECIAL NOTE: Have you ever wondered where the phrase, "Yes, Virginia..." comes from. Well, I did, so here is the scoop as we say in the journalism field. "Yes, Virginia, there is a Santa Claus" is a line from an editorial published in *The Sun* newspaper on September 21, 1897 in New York City. The author was writer Francis Church, and he was responding to a letter by eight-year-old Virginia O'Hanlon asking whether Santa Claus was real. She had doubts that came from several of her friends questioning Santa's existence. Here's part of his response. "Virginia, your little friends are wrong. They have been affected by the skepticism of a skeptical age." He continued to write that Santa Claus existed "as certainly as love and generosity and devotion exist" and that the world would be "dreary" if he did not. Church argued that just because something could not be seen did not mean it was not real. "Nobody can conceive or imagine all the wonders there are unseen and unseeable in the world." He concluded that "you may tear apart the baby's rattle and see what makes the noise inside, but there is a veil covering the unseen world which not the strongest men that ever lived, could tear apart. Only faith, fancy, poetry, love, romance, can push aside that curtain and view and picture the supernal beauty and glory beyond. Is it all real? Ah, VIRGINIA, in all this world there is nothing else real and abiding. No Santa Claus? Thank God! He lives and he lives forever. A thousand years from now, Virginia, nay, ten times ten thousand years from now, he will continue to make glad the heart of childhood."

CHAPTER 5

Letters to Santa

Over these past almost three decades, I have received hundreds and hundreds of letters from children. Most have been personally hand delivered by kids clenching their best works in writing. Sometimes the letters were delivered by parents and grandparents if the children were home "under the weather" or unable to attend in person. When I searched through those shoeboxes I mentioned, I totaled up over six hundred. There were also just over two hundred hand drawn pictures, some with glitter, cotton balls to simulate snow and other very creative artwork. I wrote the location, name, and age of each child on the envelopes. Every time I moved around the country, I was tempted to discard all of them, but I just could not bring myself to do it. This must have been the reason! Plus, on any dreary day, I could always open one of the boxes and it would change my whole demeanor. Here are some of my favorites for you.

From Susie, 9, at a Police department reserves children's party. "I made a copy of this letter that I'm giving to you today and mailed it to the North Pole. Due to your advanced age and all of your travels, I wanted to make sure it didn't get lost between here and the Elves' workshop. I must declare that I have been as close to perfect this whole year as I could be. My three brothers and their out-of-control puppy, not so much. But I'll let them try to defend themselves to you, good luck with that!!! I'm planning to be an attorney when I get older, so I'm thinking that a laptop would be a great gift this year. It can be a reasonably priced one, not top of the line. I know you need to spread your budget around. Well that kind of sums it up. You might want to start taking those brain supplements I see on TV every day, just saying. Please give Mrs. Claus and all of the Elves and Reindeer my love. Susie"

From Ethan, 7, at a Boys & Girls Club holiday party. "Hey Santa, what's up? My name is Ethan and I been a pretty good guy in the year you know. I even promise to be super better next year if that helps this time around. I like school, mostly recess, naptime, and lunch. It would be really cool if I could get a snake for Christmas. I'd hide him under my bed so no one will know. Really, I promise, I'd even find him rats and stuff to eat. So, I don't forget, if my older sister writes you stuff about me don't believe her cause she's like always on my case. Women, wow, my dad's right. OK, that's all for now. Don't get too tired out flying all around OK, I put our address again on here, so you don't end up next door. I don't think they like snakes. Bye for now, your best buddy in the world, Ethan."

I included this next story from Volume one because it involves a letter. A young boy and girl came up to Santa with their mom at a base military recreation center and handed Santa a letter. They asked Santa if he could deliver it to their daddy in Heaven when he was flying by. Mom explained to Santa that her husband had passed away recently due to combat injuries. The kids said they wanted their daddy to know that they loved him. Santa assured the children that he would make sure to stop there on his rounds Christmas Eve. The two looked at their mommy, she smiled and said thanks. As they turned and walked away, the little girl turned back around and said, "It's OK if Jesus wants to read it too." I also picked this letter as my favorite heartwarming story, so you'll read it elsewhere in this book. I still wanted to share it here. Thanks for bearing with me.

Grace, 6, came up to Santa at a church hall holiday party. She had been pacing back and forth in front of the stage for quite a while. I knew she was trying to get her courage up, so I tried to make eye contact and smile at her the best I could while seeing other children. Finally, she made her big move. She came up and stood right in front of me. She looked up, handed me a letter, and blurted out, "This is from my brother Chase, he's got the flu and it's really gross. I don't know what's in it and so I don't wanna' be in trouble with his bad deeds, OK?" I assured her that his letter and her visit would be totally separate. She was very relieved about that. "I didn't sleep all night worrying 'bout this you know." I again reassured her that all was good. When she left, I looked down at the envelope which had strawberry jam stains on one side, and Santa spelled "Santtas." I could not wait to read what was inside!

Brandon, 8, came to see Santa at his local Fire department station children's party. He handed me a 9 X 12 manila envelope. Taped to the top was also a return envelope addressed to him with a stamp attached. I just knew this was going to be good! "Hey, Merry Christmas Santa, well, actually it's not Christmas yet, but you know what I mean," he said. "I've researched a couple of ideas for presents for me, I mean I've been pretty darn good if I say so myself," he added. Before I could speak, he said, "So, I printed out all of the information on each one from the internet, with pix and stuff, so it's easy for your guys up there at the North Pole." I told him I would certainly take a good look at everything and appreciated all of his hard work in putting together the packet. "I'm really a whiz on the computer, do you know how to work one or does your IT department handle that, he asked?" I told him Mrs. Claus was our North Pole tech genius. He smiled and added, "Figures, plus I added a self-addressed envelope in case she needs to have me provide more details on anything." He then added, "I can imagine this can be a real major worldwide project." I assured him his wish packet was in good hands. He smiled again, turned to leave, looked back around, and said, "Next year how 'bout a Santa letter app!"

Elizabeth, 5, came up at her local pre-school children's party and sat on Santa's knee. She lifted my beard as lots of kids do. She said, "Huh, soft." She was holding a letter in her hand and held onto it very tight. She looked straight into my eyes and said, "Here's my letter, I's little so if I goofed up, sorry Santa, please still love me, OK?" I told her that Santa would always love her no matter what. I asked her what her age was, and she replied, "5 and a quarter, so almost 6." She added, "My older sister wrote her letter on her 'puter so it's better, huh?" I assured her that any kind of letter to Santa is a good letter. She smiled, stoked my beard, jumped down and ran off to her mom who was standing nearby. Her mom smiled and leaned down by my ear to tell me her daughter had been so very nervous about writing her first letter to Santa. After they both left, I looked down at the envelope and it said, "I love you Santa" with a very cute drawing of a heart and a gingerbread house with her at the front door.

Erik, 7, stopped to see Santa Claus at a neighborhood kids Christmas party. He had his Christmas wish list letter in his front pocket which was now pretty wrinkled up. He was wearing a T-shirt from the hit movie "Elf," starring Will Farrell, with the phrase, 'SANTA, I KNOW HIM!!!' He blurted out, "Hope you're ready for me, everybody says I'm a real handful. Actually, people say lots of other stuff 'bout me too but there's lots of families here so I won't repeat it." I just smiled and said, "What's on your mind young man?" He looked at me and replied, "You really want to know, wow, that's a first." "I wore this T-shirt 'cause I thought it would be a good icebreaker, what 'ya think Santa?" I just smiled again and said he had pretty good taste in movies. He pulled out his letter, tried to flatten it out a bit and handed it to me. He looked a little sheepish and said, "Sorry 'bout this, I was skateboardin' over here and well, it got a little bent and stuff." I assured him, bent or not, it was the effort that counted. He wiped his brow and replied, "Oh good, 'cause I'm known for really screwing things up if you know what I mean." He added, "'Course, you probably already know that. OK, my work here is done," he added as he walked away. He turned, and said, "Merry Christmas!" I looked down at the envelope which had a drawing of Santa Claus on a skateboard with the phrase 'SANTA DUDE.' Oh, the letter, well, let's just say it was creative and he was looking for a pet alligator, a skateboard park in his backyard, a red Camaro convertible for when he turned 16, a date with Britney Spears and … well, you can only imagine, it was four pages long!

A special one for me was a letter given to me by a little girl and boy at a wildfire relief temporary housing shelter. It had a drawing on the front in crayon with a sleigh and reindeer. Inside was a very simple message. "Please Santa, we would love to have anything you can give our family right now. Thank you, your friends, Sarah, and Braden."

CHAPTER 6

Hold Your Children Close

O ne day, I left my home in Makaha Valley, on the far west end of the leeward side of the island of Oahu to drive to Kapolei. Makaha is on the Waianae Coast, a rural oceanside area. It has been my home these past 3 years after many years in Las Vegas and lots of different states on the mainland.

As I drove on Farrington Highway, the only way in and out of the region, there was a large rally going on with adults and children lining the roadway with signs. Most signs read, "Save our Keiki" (kids/children), "Protect our Children" and "Help Save our Keiki." There also were donation baskets held by long poles for drivers and passengers to reach out of their vehicles and put some funds in. I had to stop and understand what was going on. In talking with one mom, she explained that human trafficking was a real issue in the islands and particularly on Oahu, the most populous of the islands with over 900, 000 residents. She educated me on the entire matter. It opened my eyes in many ways. I stayed up on most major issues in the islands especially with Hawaii Public Radio and Hawaii PBS, but this one had not been top of mind for me. I left my donation and went on my way. It stayed with me from that day.

In mid-December, I made Santa visits to several women's and children's shelters on the islands. There is a full chapter on these visits as well in Chapter 16. In each case before visiting with those gathered, the staff fills me in on the situation I will be dealing with. Verbal and physical abuse and abandonment are the most typical.

In one particular situation, I was going to visit a mom and her four children. The kids ranged in age from 2 to 7 years old. It turned out that their dad was dealing with a serious opioid addiction and had arranged to sell the children to human traffickers on the mainland to feed his habit. He had made a mistake and told the oldest child that they were going to go on a "airplane ride." The boy told his mom and a verbal and physical incident followed with her husband. Fortunately, she was able to gather the kids together and flee their home and find shelter.

The children were not fully aware of all that had happened and how close they came to being separated from their island home and family. I decided to just provide as much fun, laughter, and distraction that I could. Typically, I stay with each family for a half hour or so, but in this case, it went well over an hour. We read a book, played two games, and passed out a few small gifts to each child plus my customary large candy cane. I spent some extra time just with mom trying to give her some comfort, hope and encouragement.

I finished up the afternoon and evening shelter visits, changed out of the Santa suit and got on the H1 freeway for the drive home. I got about halfway home and had to pull over onto the shoulder of the highway to pull myself together. I struggled with my feelings thinking about the shelter visit and back to those Farrington highway rally attendees and their signs.

Two days later I had a late morning Breakfast with Santa, then a special Santa stop for a close friend's great granddaughters first birthday celebration. I finished the day with my second annual Santa visit for the grandchildren of close friends in Manoa. There are some really funny things that happened at the first visit which are featured in Chapter 23, "It Can Only Happen to Santa!" As this day closed, I was filled with joy and happiness.

My drive home from my friend's home in Manoa is 40 miles and usually takes about an hour and fifteen/twenty minutes. This night was to be quite different. I was driving on H1, a freeway. I made it to the airport exit area (10 miles) before I had to pull off on the shoulder. What hit me was the contrast between the situation of the family in the shelter and the families of my close friends. It could not have been more different. The contrast was so very stark to me. I finally pulled myself together and went on. I only made it to the Ewa exit, (9 miles) and it happened again. I pulled off the freeway onto the shoulder again to get it together. It felt like I would never make it all the way home. I just couldn't shake the feelings I had. I wrote down all that was going on inside my head, hence this chapter. The plan between my friends and I, when I make the drive home late at night, is to text them when I have arrived safely back in Makaha. Since it had already been an hour and twnety minutes and I was only halfway home, I texted and said all was good so they would not be concerned. It was just a little white lie, right?

As I finally came around the bend into the Nanakuli/Waianae area of the Waianae Coast on Farrington highway, I thought back to the rally, the messages on the signs and how real the entire crisis of human trafficking is. It had left a very deep impact and impression on me. I felt I needed to share it with you.

So, hold your children close, treasure your family time, and enjoy each and every day you all have together. Celebrate family! (Ohana)

CHAPTER 7

Santa in Paradise

My first 26 years being Santa Claus were on the mainland United States in eight different states. The past 2 years and going forward are in Hawaii as well as returning to the West Coast as needed for wildfire temporary housing Santa visits. Being Santa Claus in Hawaii is the same and yet quite different all at the same time. Hawaii is the 50th state of the United States and was its own island nation which means having its own language, customs, traditions and so much more. And the weather...

Being born and raised in Wisconsin, I was used to the winter cold and snow, lots, and lots of snow. I remember reminiscing recently with my older brother Jim about those days. Several years there simply was nowhere to shovel the snow to. Jim had the misfortune of being inside a snow igloo we made when it collapsed on him. I was once pinned in a snowbank while delivering the huge Sunday morning newspapers when my bike fell sideways. Later I lived and worked in Lake Tahoe and Reno for 12 years. In March 1991, while in Lake Tahoe, it snowed twenty feet in one month. I recall the day I walked home from work, as the roads were closed, and was unable to get in my front door. I climbed up the snowbank to the second level, where fortunately, I had left a patio door unlocked.

Moving around the country most of my adult life, I got used to all kinds of different climates. However, nothing prepares you to be Santa Claus in the wonderful South Pacific!

It does snow in Hawaii, yes it does. On the summits of the three tallest volcanoes, Mauna Kea, (13, 796 feet above sea level, 33, 000 feet total) Mauna Loa (13, 678 feet above sea level) and Haleakala, (10, 023 feet above sea level) it snows. The record is two feet of snow in December 2016 on Mauna Kea.

My very first Christmas in Hawaii was as a visitor on the islands of Kauai and Maui about 20 years ago. I always read the local news-papers and websites when I travel so that I can participate in local events and meet the locals. That meant attending a wonderful slack key guitar Christmas concert under the stars on Kauai. It also meant watching festive decorated outriggers in Maui. All of the islands in the Hawaiian island chain have their own distinctive celebrations. Boats at all the marinas are decorated. In Honolulu, on Oahu Island, a giant Santa ("Shaka" Santa) and Mrs. Claus (Tutu Mele), decked out in a combination of traditional and island wear, sit at the entrance to Honolulu Hale, the seat of City/County government. A 50-foot Norfolk Pine tree is lit up there in a special ceremony. It is also the location for Honolulu City Lights. During the pandemic, the light show was moved to the parking lot of Aloha Stadium for a drive-thru experience. Hotels and resorts throughout the islands are decorated to the max. Famed Waikiki Santa, now passed away, came in by outrigger and read the "Nice List" on the famed Waikiki beach accompanied by traditional hula dancers, (how come I never get hula dancers?). Santa, arriving by red canoe accompanied by dolphins, is also something to see. Santa's also arrive on surfboards along the Waikiki beaches. Red and green shave ice is everywhere, red, and green sugar coating for malasada's add to that amazing Portuguese donut treat. Did I mention the fireworks? Red and green fireworks go off all over during the week of Christmas, all the way through New Year's Day. Actually, on the Waianae Coast where I live, it keeps going long after New Year's!

Christmas in the islands is a treasured holiday. Traditional Norfolk Pine Christmas trees, as well as several other varieties, can be found at Helemano Farms on Oahu Island. The rest are shipped from Oregon, Washington State, and other mainland states. If families cannot get one, palm trees are decorated instead. Amazing, almost tree-size Poinsettias, bloom right about Christmas Day. Santa is actually Kana Kaloka. I enjoy musical group Na Leo singing "Here Comes Santa Claus." Traditionally, pre-Christmas is Makahiki, a three-four-month period celebrating well wishes, giving thanks and gifts to loved ones wishing peace and good will. Christmas eve is Ahiahi Kalikimaka and Merry Christmas is Mele Kalikimaka.

Christmas feasts (Luaus) feature traditional holiday foods like ham, turkey, and roasts with all the trimmings, but island favorites like kalua pork, sticky rice, poi, poke, lomi lomi salmon, lau lau and famed North Shore bakery Ted's Haupia pie are all enjoyed by festive Ohana (families). Songs break out spontaneously and ukuleles are everywhere. Church services, special events and activities abound. Special holiday leis are worn, and surfers wade out wearing Santa caps. Hot chocolate is enjoyed while the air conditioner is blasting. Islanders wear everything from holiday hoodies and shorts, ugly sweaters, and swimsuits.

Homes are festively decorated; Christmas Tree Lane in Kaneohe on Oahu Island is something to see. Community parades are held in every town on every island. It seems like every truck on the islands is decorated with wreaths, lights, and reindeer horns!

Snowmen are replaced by sandmen. Bad weather concerns never enter the picture at all. Menehunes replace elves, Santa's wear festive tropical shirts, rolled up red pants and slippers (flip flops). The Holiday Hula's are absolutely spectacular. Everything has a tropical flair to it.

Christmas music is also unique with Bing Crosby's "12 Days of Christmas" done Hawaiian style by various artists. His version of "Mele Kalikimaka" is very popular. "O Holy Night," sung by Maui's favorite son Uncle Willy K, is special. Everyone's favorite island comedian, Frank DeLima, joins the Honolulu Boys Choir for "No Mo' Christmas Blues" all about that infamous "Naughty List." "Po La'ie, (Silent Night), featuring Don Ho and Tia Carrere, is very moving, Leonard Kwan's slack key guitar "We Wish You a Merry Christmas" is wonderful. So many more, I could fill the rest of the book. The islands are all about mele (music) and I love it!

So, what is different for Santa Claus? How long have you got...? First is the costume itself. Yes Virginia, it does get warm in there. Lots of Santa visits are held outdoors where the temperature averages eighty in December. It is being in the direct sunlight that can be the most challenging. I always have had two full Santa suits for each appearance. In Hawaii, I added a third one. I have often had to change out several times in one day for multiple events. The dry cleaner and I are on a first name basis! There are also blue Santa suits everywhere to fit into the islands. Many Surfin' Santa's wear Santa caps with rolled up pants or shorts and no boots. Everything works!

The Christmas gift wishes from children are also different and fun. One of the most sought after are Zippy's Gift cards, a popular local restaurant chain.

The tradition of leaving milk and cookies for Santa is also some-what different. Malasadas often replace the cookies. A little girl told me she would leave a plate of them for me, but she could not guarantee that her twin brother would not take a few bites out of them. A 7-year-old boy told me he would leave me a Bikini Blonde, instead of milk, which is a local beer produced by Maui Brewing Company. I have been promised freshly made Mai Tai's, Longboard and Big Wave beers from Kona Brewing Company plus some of that delicious Koloa Island rum. One Tutu (grand-mother) was with her twin grandsons and promised me a piping hot bowl of Portuguese bean soup! A little girl told me that she would leave me "a whole lot of poi, 'cause I don't like it."

Another challenge for Santa is listening to the wishes of a local youngster talking in 'pidgin, ' a popular island slang language. I always make sure I get the correct interpretation from da' elf!

I will close this chapter out with a story from my previous book. It's all about being homesick for Christmas in Hawaii.

At a military base children's Christmas party on the west coast of the mainland, a 7-year-old boy was introduced to Santa by the Head Elf as Kyle from Kailua. His family had just relocated. His dad was deployed to the middle east and his mom was working. As he stood there on the stage with a sad look on his face, Santa dis-played the double "Shaka" sign and said, "Aloha Kyle from Kailua, Mele Kalikimaka!" (Hello Kyle from Kailua, Merry Christmas) The boy's eyes got extra wide, his jaw dropped almost to the floor, he stared at Santa for ten seconds before finally saying, "OMG, OMG, OMG!" He leaned in and gave Santa a big bear hug, not wanting to let go. Santa told Kyle he knew exactly where Kailua was, (Oahu Island, Hawaii) and that he loved flying his sleigh to all of the islands. Kyle finished giving Santa his Christmas wish list, then sat on the stage near Santa for another hour. When it was time to go, Kyle flashed the double "Shaka" sign, smiled a huge, wide smile and waved goodbye to Santa. Santa returned the "Shaka" sign and again wished Kyle "Mele Kalikimaka." As the boy walked away, the Head Elf told Santa that he knew the boy's family and Kyle had looked so sad when he first came into the recreation center that afternoon. And that, my friends, is what Christmas is all about for me.

CHAPTER 8

Questions and Answers: The Q & A Session with Santa

Over the decades, I have been asked numerous questions about the role of Santa, plus my insights into portraying the role. I hope these will answer some of those questions.

I am often asked what the most amazing place is that I have been Santa at. There are a dozen really fascinating and meaningful situations that immediately come to mind. However, if I have to pick just one, it will have to be for the Pueblo of Acoma in New Mexico at their ancestral site, "the Rock" located on a 365+ foot mesa. Acoma "Sky City" is the oldest continuously inhabited community in North America. I had the honor and pleasure of being Director of Marketing for Acoma Business Enterprises, the Pueblo's business entity, for three and a half years. They hosted Christmas Eve and Christmas Day special events for Pueblo families and friends. Several hundred children had gathered for Christmas Day services at their 16th century Mission. I arrived on the back of the Pueblo's fire truck (with the EMT unit following). There in the Spanish Mission, I presented blankets to the Matriarchs of the thirteen clans, presented a plate of food at the altar and caught my Santa sleeve on the hand of the hand carved wooden Christ child, which had been presented to the Pueblo by the King of Spain (which is in itself a whole other story). I presented plates of fruits and nuts to the Pueblo Elders and War Chiefs around a traditional bonfire. Later I visited with and gave presents to about two hundred children of the Pueblo's families. Photos were taken plus treats handed out. I knew dozens and dozens of the families although none "knew" me. The bright faces, big smiles, laughter, sibling teasing and delight from receiving candy and presents was contagious. Four hours had passed quickly. I climbed on back of the fire truck, waved goodbye and got down to the base of the mesa. I then climbed in the passenger seat of the truck for the ride back. Santa always has to be careful with his public persona. The desire to get out of the suit after a lengthy period, yes, it is hot in there, is tempting. You just cannot risk taking off any part of the full costume. On this day, as Santa made his way in the Fire Station to the restroom to change, sure enough, two special needs children who had not made it to "the rock" were waiting at the fire station. We spent some time together and they left with their parents, thrilled that they were able to meet Santa. Then the change out to my "civies." Before I left the volunteer Fire Station, one of the firefighters, whom I had known for several years, said, "How do you do that up there all day long?" I told him I never really thought about it, I just do it. Just like he volunteers to help keep his community safe. It was a long, meaningful & magical day. I did find time later to write down a dozen stories of what children had said to me. This was one of those days in our lives that makes it all worthwhile and keeps you pushing forward. Several months later I received a Special Commendation certificate from the Pueblo Governor to: Don Kennedy (Santa Claus). It meant a great deal to me. For me, Santa is a figure of hope, happiness, goodness, and kindness. Even in the face of fear, despair, and tragedy, he needs to provide comfort, good cheer, and peace, especially to those who in need.

Another question I get constantly is how Santa does not cry or laugh at the amazing comments and stories kids share. It is important that Santa remains an anonymous, independent, non-judgmental sounding board for kids so that they feel safe, secure, and open to sharing. My secret, which I have shared with the elves, if all else fails, is to bite the inside of my cheek if it gets really hard to contain my reaction and emotions. Sometime at the end of a long day, I feel like I have been to the dentist. Yes, I have gone home numerous times that way! I also tell elves to just turn away and let their emotions out which, of course, does not work for Santa directly facing a child.

How many Santa suits does St. Nick go through in a season? Yes, accidents do happen, and Santa does need to be prepared. I always keep a second suit with me for just those "occasions." A typical Holiday Season is 1 or 2 suits.

How much does a quality Santa suit cost? About $500 total.

What are some of the kinds of accidents that have occurred? Trust me, you do not want to know, just use your imagination and we will leave it at that!

How many times does Santa get his beard pulled? I have finally stopped counting!

A question that often comes up is what to do if a child says something that may indicate problems or issues at home. This has happened several dozen times over the years. I was trained to share this discreetly with the organizers of the appearance who can then follow up with the correct authorities who deal with these situations.

How perceptive are children with Santa? In addition to lifting up his beard and watching for Santa's exit for a glimpse of the sleigh and reindeer, here are two of my favorites. I had been Santa for the Primm Valley Casino Resorts employees' children's holiday parties and employee housing parties for many years. Lots and lots of the same kids attended each year and I treasured watching them grow up. I had not always worn the white gloves I do now. I have been wearing a fairly distinctive watch and ring on my left hand for a long time. One year a little girl sat on my lap as she always did and pointed to my watch and ring and declared, "I'm glad it's you again, the real Santa, cause there's lots of fake ones out there, you know." A fellow Santa from a sheriff's department in Florida told me of a similar occurrence. He had a role as "Officer Friendly" visiting elementary schools in his county. The kids would all sit on the floor as he talked with them. He typically visited each school at least twice each year. One day, in his role as Santa Claus, a little girl whispered in his ear and said, "I know who you are, you're Officer Friendly." Santa was surprised and said, "Yes, I'm one of Santa's helpers, how did you know." She pointed to his distinctive work boots and replied, "Those are Officer Friendly's shoes." Sitting on the floor several times each year, she had noticed his boots.

What was it like to be Santa Claus during the height of the pandemic? I did portray Santa during the two Christmas holiday seasons during the pandemic. I wrote a chapter in this book all about it.

How emotional can the more heartwarming stories be? A former Vice President of mine was sitting on the couch at her home when her husband came home and was concerned that she was crying. She replied, "It's ok, I'm just reading Don's book." In a similar vein, a former General Manager of mine came into my office one day and said, "You made me cry at my desk, Don." I had given him a copy of my first book. Typically, not the best idea to make your bosses cry!!!

What was it like moving to Hawaii and being Santa there? I have been Santa in eight states over the years, but Hawaii was a unique experience. I wrote a chapter in this book on being Santa in paradise.

The question I get asked the most is how I got started portraying Santa. The full explanation is in the second chapter, The Very First Time. Second most asked question is why I continue, plus, why I did not stop after the 25-year mark. The reasons are many, but mainly it became a passion of mine. Even though I was twice married, I have no children. So, being able to share six weeks each year with hundreds and hundreds of children is a blessing. There is such a need, I just have to do my small part to help fill it. I kept going after the quarter century mark because I started getting emails and calls in year 26 and figured what is another year. Then another, then another. I have decided to keep going as long as I physically, mentally, and emotionally can.

What is the most special thing for me as Santa? Holding a newborn and being part of their first Christmas. Even though I have nieces and nephews, holding the precious child of parents is almost too much for me. Especially if I know the family. I am in awe to begin with, then there are the glasses, long hair, long, full beard, everything in the way of seeing well. Carefully supporting the head and neck of a newborn is so important. The youngest I have had the honor of holding is the daughter of my close friends Juli and Stephen Slocum. Isabelle, "Izzy" was eight weeks old when she came to visit me at the Boys and Girls Club of Southern Highlands in Las Vegas. After that I was able to be her Santa several more times, I loved watching her grow up. I have held and been Santa for hundreds of children in their first year and treasure every single time.

Why did you include lots of sad stories instead of just all funny stories? I actually started out just writing all funny stories, but as I had sifted through all of the accumulated decades of stories, I realized that some of the most memorable ones were not funny at all. Instead, they were heartwarming and sometime heart wrenching. So, I changed the entire theme of the first book in mid-writing.

Did you write the book just for adults? Yes, I did, but now it turns out children are reading them. I wish I had thought that all through at the beginning. Children can read a lot of the actual stories, but some of the writing is still geared more for adults.

What are the most fun things brought to you at Santa appearances? Wow, how much space do we have for that? Cash, a little boy with his mom's checkbook, the proverbial brown paper sack with a flask of bourbon, but my favorites are the hand drawn artwork, so precious.

What is it like to put on the whole Santa outfit? It is far more involved than I ever imagined. I have never been a GQ person, so pulling myself together in regular life is a real project. Laying out glasses, gloves, belt, boots, socks, undergear, coat, pants, beard, hair, (I truly envy Santa's that can grow their own) the spare suit, duffle bags, suitcases, eyebrow whitener, hairbrush, clothes, shoes, etc. for after-Santa... shower availability, towel, where to secure your wallet, watch, car keys and other personal items. It is a project to say the least!

What was the biggest surprise in your writing? I think it is the worldwide reach today, especially of eBooks. As mentioned earlier, the very first eBook read was in Sydney, Australia. I have received feedback from all over the globe. The other surprise was the interest from libraries and book clubs.

Another question constantly asked is for my favorite humorous and heartwarming stories. Hence, this collection of 25 years of

Santa stories. The three books I have written have over seven hundred stories plus dozens more interspersed in various sections like Letters to Santa, the First Time, etc. I truly hope you will find some personal favorites in your reading. Plus, I also hope it will cause you to recall your own favorites in your life.

If you had to pick one funny story, what would it be? Ok, the moment of truth. It is so awfully hard as there are numerous absolutely laugh-out-loud, hilarious stories. But one that always brings a smile to my face is the one I named, "The Pisgetti Story." If you have Volume 1, look at the back cover photo of the little guy in blue. If you look carefully, you can see a faint orange ring around his mouth. So, here is that story. A little boy came up with his mom at a Boys and Girls Club children's holiday party. He had an orange circle all the way around his mouth. His mom said, "Tell Santa why you have orange color all around your mouth." He looked up and said, "'Cause I was eating pisgetti!" "Spaghetti," she corrected him. "And someone was in too big of a hurry to get here so he didn't wash up," she continued. I could sense he was on the hot seat. Santa smiled and said, "I like pisgetti too." The little guy got all excited and said, "See, Santa 'nounces it like me too." His mom corrected him again, "Pronounces." The little boy leaned in close to Santa's ear and said, "I just can't win with her."

And your pick for your most heartwarming story? Wow, same thing. So very many sweet, touching, heart-tugging stories. Picking one is almost impossible, but here goes. This is also from Volume 1. A young boy and girl came up to Santa with their mom at a military base recreation center and handed Santa a letter. They asked Santa if he could deliver it to their daddy in Heaven when he was flying by. Mom explained that her husband had passed recently due to combat injuries. The kids said they wanted their daddy to know that they loved him. The little girl added, "It's OK if Jesus wants to read it too."

CHAPTER 9

Santa Claus Around the Globe

I love feedback, you never know when you are going to get some great ideas and input. In this case, it is about the various names for Santa Claus and the myriad of traditions and customs surrounding Christmas all around the world. Santa Claus, Santa, Father Christmas, St. Nicholas, Kris Kringle, St. Nick, and so many more names have been part of that history. I received several dozen or so questions about this entire subject over the past several years, so I did some research and will share that with you.

What piqued my personal interest in particular were two letters/ messages that I received.

It all started several years ago with this message I received from Albert McCarthy of Malta. Do you know where the island of Malta is? I did not, but I do now. The island is located on the European continent, just south of Sicily (Italy) in the Mediterranean Sea. The Republic of Malta, an island-state, consists of three islands with a total population of 440, 000. I am an author on Goodreads, the top online book review and recommendation website with over ninety million members worldwide. On it, readers and authors can communicate, ask questions, get answers, etc. Once readers finish reading your book, they can simply rate it on a scale of 1 to 5 and/or review it. I received this message from Albert in August of 2020. "I just finished reading your book and gave it five stars. I should know, I actually am the 'official' MALTA SANTA KLAWS. When you perform something for charity, the return is greater than cash. Go on Don, more and more children need you." If you Google him, you can read all about his incredible life's journey amid numerous challenges. I was so touched and humbled by his message. It brought me back to why I began doing what I do each holiday season. Right about the time when I received his message, I was already getting requests to schedule Santa appearances for that December. I had almost decided to retire from that role. Once in a while in life, I believe we need to be reminded of some of our mission and purpose. So, I decided to "go on, Don" as Albert put it, as long as I am able to. I mean, who can argue with the REAL SANTA KLAWS, right? His message also provided me with an example of another name for the iconic Santa Claus.

The next example was a letter from Captain Frank van der Hoeven, Master of Holland America's MS Zuiderdam. I am sailing on the ship as I write this in late April of 2022. I had sent the captain a copy of volume 2 as a small gift. This is his reply which also goes to the names and traditions subject. "Dear Mr. Don Kennedy, I'd like to take the opportunity to thank you for your kind gift and the joining letter. Although decades ago, I can imagine how young kids would react and say things when they are invited to sit on Santa's lap. My experience and that of my daughters when they had that young age, is of similar nature. The only difference was that according to Dutch tradition, we have St. Nicolaus that gives us presents on December 5th each year. Christmas celebration was much smaller in the old days but has gained commercial interest. It has and likely never be to the extent as it's celebrated in North America or EU as an example. In recent years St. Nicolaus celebration has created diversity within our country because of the old tradition of his helper 'Black Piet.' I'd not be surprised when this all goes away and Santa or 'Kerstmas' in Dutch, takes his place. Please keep writing and be that good character for the youngest generation for years to come. Thanks." Captain Frank van der Hoeven.

Saint or St. Nicolas is also spelled Nicholas and Nickolas over the years.

I was now interested in learning more. I found a wonderful, informative book when it comes to the history of Santa Claus. *Santa Claus Worldwide, A History of St. Nicholas and Other Holiday Gift-Bringers* was written by Tom A. Jerman. It's considered the best and I highly recommend it.

That history is fascinating and endless.

The consensus is that a poem that was written in 1822 by Clement C. Moore and published in 1823 in the city newspaper of Troy, New York, set in place what is now the modern universally accepted version of Santa Claus. It is called, *'Twas the Night Before Christmas,* also *A Visit from St. Nicholas,* and *The Night Before Christmas.* The poem has evolved as well, and this is one of the more recent versions of it.

'Twas the night before Christmas and all through the house, not a creature was stirring, not even a mouse. The stockings were hung by the chimney with care, in the hopes that St. Nicholas soon would be there. The children were nestled all snug in their beds, while visions of sugar plums danced in their heads. Mom in her kerchief and I in my cap, had just settled in for a long winter's nap. When out on the lawn there arose such a clatter, I sprang from my bed to see what was the matter. Away to the window I flew with a flash, tore open the shutters and threw up the sash. The moon on the breast of the new fallen snow, gave a luster of mid-day to objects below. When what to my wondering eyes should appear, but a miniature sleigh and eight tiny reindeer. With a little old driver so lively and quick, well I knew in a moment it must be St. Nick. More rapid than eagles, his coursers they came, and he whistled, and he shouted, and he called out their name.

"On Dasher, on Dancer, on Prancer and Vixen, on Comet, on Cupid, on Donner and Blitzen! To the top of the porch, to the top of the wall, now dash away, dash away, dash away all!" As dry leaves that before the wild hurricane fly, when they meet to an obstacle mount to the sky. So up to the rooftop the coursers they flew, with a sleigh full of toys and St. Nicholas too. And then in a twinkling I heard on the roof, the prancing, the pawing of each little hoof. As I drew in my head and was turning around, down the chimney St. Nicholas came with a bound. He was dressed in all fur from his head to his foot, and his clothes were all tarnished with ashes and soot. A bundle of toys he had flung on his back, and he looked like a peddler just opening his pack. His eyes how they twinkled, his dimples, how merry, his cheeks were like roses, his nose like a cherry. His droll little mouth was drawn up in a bow, and the beard on his chin was as white as the snow. The stump of his pipe, he held tight in his teeth, and the smoke, it encircled his head like a wreath. He had a broad face and a little round belly, that shook when he laughed (ho, ho, ho) like a bowl full of jelly (ho, ho, ho).

He was chubby and plump, a right jolly old elf, and I laughed when I saw him in spite of myself. A wink of his eye, and a twist of his head, soon gave me to know I had nothing to dread. He spoke not a word, but went straight to his work, and filled all the stockings and turned with a jerk. And laying a finger to the side of his nose and giving a nod up the chimney he rose. He sprang to the sleigh, and to his team gave a whistle, and away they all flew like the down of a thistle. But I heard him exclaim as he drove out of sight, "Merry Christmas to all and to all a goodnight!"

The accepted historical beginning of today's modern Santa Claus is that of St. Nicholas, of which there were two, one being the patron saint of children. Prior to that there was St. Martin. It was all based on the practice of winter solstice gift giving. Gift givers and bringers began in Europe in the Middle Ages. In addition to this, charitable gift giving became popular during the holiday seasons. Around the globe, there are numerous figures that filled the role, plus countless meaningful holiday traditions. Gift giving today occurs between November 11 and January 6. Early characters, some continuing to this day, include Weinachmann, Pe're Noel, Ded Moroz, Christkindl, Sinterklass, Belsnickle, Knecht Ruprecht, Snegurochka, Le Befana, the 3 Kings, the Christ Child and Grandfather Frost are just some. Old Santa Claus became just Santa Claus or Santa. He was and continues to be a constantly changing, and evolving, adapting, cultural figure. Yule goats and gnomes evolved into elves. In the America's, the early 1930's Coca Cola print ads, and later commercials, featuring Santa, really cemented the public's perception of modern Santa Claus. Another key moment in modern history is that of famed illustrator Norman Rockwell's covers of Santa Claus in the Saturday Evening Post in the 1920's. I could fill an entire book about what I have learned, but that has already been done. I hope this helps answer some questions.

One fun story was shared with me by a family friend which relates to the various names and children's fascination with jolly old Saint Nick. A little boy, who was just old enough to begin understanding the Christmas holidays, was busily opening, and closing every closet door in his house, upstairs and downstairs. Then, he would start all over again. Finally, his mom had to ask him what he was doing. He replied, "I keep hearing 'bout Santa closet and I can't find him anywhere," he replied in exasperation. His mom explained to him that it was "Santa Claus, not Santa closet." Ah, as usual, mom to the rescue, mystery solved!

CHAPTER 10

Santa in a pandemic

I have been through all kinds of things as Santa Claus over these many years, but nothing prepared me for the Covid-19 pandemic and aftermath. Trying to balance being safe and healthy, while still visiting children during those two holiday seasons, was challenging to say the least.

My Santa visits were cut in half, and I worked closely with event organizers to keep things as safe as possible for all involved. Lots of social distancing, masks (many festive and creative), tons of hand sanitizers, constant hand washing, some plastic shields, etc. The large candy canes I give away at each event are wrapped individually in plastic so that was helpful. One less thing to worry about. If there is a will, there is a way became our motto. I got an additional Santa suit, the fourth, so that I could rotate them in and out of the dry cleaner. I washed my beard and hair several times each week and wore new white gloves each time. I home tested twice a day, once in the morning and once at night. Twice weekly I did the full PCR testing. We made it!

I did want to share some cute, fun stories from that period as well. Leave it to our children to be resilient, caring, loving, kind and positive during anything that comes our way.

A little boy with an Elf facemask came up to Santa holding a plastic bag from Longs Drugs, a local pharmacy store. When he got to me, he pulled out some medical grade facemasks, a bottle of hand sanitizer and several bottles of water. He smiled, pointed to the facemasks, and said, "These are the real deal. I don't want you to get sick." He then gave me a big hug. His grandparents were with him and were so proud of him.

A girl, 6, came up wearing a reindeer mask. She stopped right in front of me and said, "I'm smiling Santa, even if you can't see it." I told her I could feel her sweet smile. "I love you, thanks for coming this time to see me," she added.

A boy, 5, stopped to visit Santa at the outdoor children's event in Makaha where I live. He was with his dad. He wore a Santa cap. He stood off at a distance and looked at me for a bit. Finally, he came closer and said, "I didn't think you'd come this year 'cause all this "coded" stuff." I smiled and assured him that "Santa would always come, no matter what." He looked up and said, "Promise?" I shook my head up and down and gave him a pinkie finger promise. He got all excited, broke out in a huge smile and turned to his dad. He declared, "Daddy, daddy, Santa will always come, forevers!"

A little girl came to see Santa at a community center holiday party. She had an Elf mask on. She held out a bottle of Flintstone vitamins, half empty, and looked very serious. "You better take these and eat all your veggies and all your fruit and stuff and not so many cookies, so you be healthy, OK?" Mom and dad beamed at their little princess. I promised her I would take good care all Christmas season.

The Makaha Valley Plantation Santa visit, referred to in the ear-lier story about the boy with the Santa cap, was held during the pandemic. Even though the housing development was built in the mid-1970's, it was a real first for the community that has 572 units. The idea arose in November. The event came together as most do, all volunteer, lots of emails, phone calls, zoom meet-ings, etc. There was lots of discussion about how to conduct the event safely. The island of Oahu had just started re-opening public spaces. Having the event outdoors helped. The location selected, also offered lots of open space for distancing. Santa arrived in a white convertible driven by a fellow resident. An elf helped get families in line and introduced them to Santa. Prizes were distributed through a raffle, and candy canes were handed out to everyone. Residents took photos with their cell phones plus an elf offered as well so everyone could be in the photo. A tent was set up by the office management with a security staff member assisting. Adults offered their assistance on the spot. Even the elf's family dog, Bonzai, was decked out in an elf costume! It all came together as if it had been planned for a year. As I walked back to my residence with them, I thought about the phrase, "it takes a village" or in this case, "it takes Ohana (family)." We can do anything when we do it together.

CHAPTER 11

Military Families

Making Santa appearances at military bases, National Guard facilities, veteran's hospitals, USO events and veteran organization's holiday parties have always had special meaning to me. Often the children attending have parents who are deployed. The children, spouses and other family members need sincere and caring answers to their many heartfelt concerns and questions. Santa also can't cross the line and make promises that are not realistic no matter how he may want to. I have had countless situations where Santa needed to provide hope in very difficult times. The recent passing of a loved one is indeed the most difficult to discuss. I studied for the ministry at Concordia College and often draw on counseling classes I had plus faith itself. Happily, I've also been able to share in reuniting families with their service member on the spot. Usually there's been great advance work done prior to the "ta-da" moment. Each feeling is very different, but all are a blessing to be part of. Very often, kids ask Santa to find room on his sleigh to return a deployed parent to them in time for the holidays. I don't think I recall more heartwarming moments than that. Children of deployed parents often carry bottled up emotions inside. I'll always remember the little boy who leaned in very close to my ear and said, "I don't want mommy to feel bad, so I don't say anything about missing my daddy." Talk about courage and caring at a young age. In talking to children about deployed parents, they often are quiet at first and then everything just comes pouring out. I've learned to do a whole lot of listening in those moments. The proud son of a World War II Army veteran, I've always had a sincere respect and appreciation for service. Serving one's state and country is indeed a special service. Selflessly leaving one's family for long and multiple periods of deployment is an even greater service. Santa's role, I've come to learn, is to provide that extra dose of hope, encouragement, comfort, warmth, fun and good cheer to these very special families in need.

Two brothers, 6 and 7, visited Santa at a military base children's Christmas party with their enlisted dad. The oldest boy spoke first and at the top of his wish list was to, "Stay in one place for a while instead of moving around all the time." Dad chuckled at that. His other son chimed in, "Sometimes you know, I don't even 'member where I am anymore." The older son replied, "That's got nothing to do with dad's job, you can get lost in our backyard!" Dad busted up, nodding his head in agreement. "I think it's best if you get him his own GPS for Christmas so we can keep track of him Santa," added the older boy. "I only get lost when I don't know where I am or where I'm going," said the younger boy in his defense. Dad finally said, "Guys, time to go, this could go on all night and Santa has a full house of kids to talk to yet." Santa reassured the boys he would be able to find them wherever their dad was stationed. They started off to enjoy the rest of the party, but Santa reminded them to get their candy cane from him first. The oldest boy looked at his brother and said in disgust, "See, you almost blew that too." Poor dad had his hands full for sure.

A boy, 6, was with his dad when he stopped to see Santa. When I asked him what he wanted to be when he grew up, he thought for a bit and finally said, "Just like my dad, a' Air Force super-hero!" His dad beamed. I asked him to explain further. He replied, "'Cause, they always get the girl!" Enough said.

A girl, 7, came up the steps at a National Guard holiday party to see Santa, stood right in front of him, put her hands on her hips and declared, "This is what you brought me last Christmas and it still doesn't fit right!" I told her that sometimes the elves do not always get things right but that I would try to do better this year. "Well, I think instead I'd rather have Mrs. Claus pick out something for me, I bet she has better fashion sense," she added. "I mean, just look at what you're wearing," she said. Ah, yes, a future fashionista in training!

A little boy was with his dad at a military base for his very first official visit with Santa. His dad had been an elf with me for several years when his son was too young to know what all was going on. His dad stood proudly by as his son leaned in and whispered, "I got a secret." I always enjoyed hearing those four words because you just never knew what was coming. His dad got a bit closer hoping to hear it as well. "So, my daddy's a spy, but I'm not 'spos-sed to tell anyone," the boy said. His dad started laughing as he was a pilot. I just had to clear this up for everyone, so I asked the boy to explain. He leaned in close again and whispered, "He told me if I was good today, we'd play I spy with my little eye." Ah, official secret mystery solved!

A little girl visited with Santa and declared, "My daddy's a 'ossifer." I asked her what rank he was. She did not understand so I added, "Do you know how important he is?" She replied, "Real important at work." Then she added, "At home, mommy's boss."

A boy, 7, stopped to visit with Santa and said he was very con-cerned about the skies these days. "There's those new rockets taking people paying millions of bucks to space and tons of satel-lites. Plus, rockets going back and forth to the space station and on top of that did you hear about all that space junk?" I told him I had read all about it. "My dad is a F35 pilot, and I worry every time he goes up there with all that going on at the same time," he added. "So, my question is, who's in charge on Christmas Eve to make sure you don't get wiped out by something flying around," he asked? I asked him if he had heard of NORAD and their tracking of Santa each year. "Oh, yea, I did, OK, I'll check it out and get back to you, write you a follow up letter," he said, a bit relieved. He looked at his young brother and said, "You know, this is serious stuff, I'm gonna' talk to dad too and figure some-thing out." His little brother, 5, looked puzzled but still replied, "Cool." Off they went to clear the skies on Christmas Eve for every little girl and boy.

A little girl came to a base Christmas party with her mom and told Santa that her daddy is in the Navy. Santa asked what her mommy did. The little girl smiled and said, "When daddy's ship comes in, she goes to meet him, and I want to hold the anchor thing, I think."

A little boy, 6, visited Santa with his older brother who was on crutches. The boy proudly declared, "That's my brother Jared, he flies in helicopters for the Navy." Santa asked how Jacob hurt himself. The boy replied, "Well, I think he either fell out or his buddies pushed him out 'cause he beat 'em at poker." Not sure if that would be in the official incident report!

A little girl, 5, came up to Santa with her mom at a military base children's holiday party. She was a bit shy at first, but finally opened up. She said her daddy "Is in 'Gearminy saving our world for us." I told her that it was wonderful that her daddy was serving his country and making everyone safe even though he was away from them. "Yes, I wish he was here 'cause I'm gonna' be 6 too," she said. Mom leaned down at that moment and said she had arranged for a Facetime call and her husband was waiting for his cue. I looked at the little girl and said, "Well, how about we get your daddy on mommy's cellphone right now and he can wish you Merry Christmas and Happy Birthday at the same time?" Her eyes opened really wide, and she clapped in glee. And there he was, thousands and thousands of miles away. Mom teared up as her daughter talked excitedly to her father. Santa waved into the phone too. When it was all over, I finished talking with the little girl and asked her for her Christmas wish list. She replied, "All done, thanks."

Two twin brothers, 7, dressed in their service fatigues, rushed up to see Santa. One was holding a pad and the other a pen. I assumed it was their wish lists. Instead, one asked the questions while the other took notes. "Sugar, peanut butter, chocolate chip cookies or some of each," said the first boy? I told him I was good with whatever variety they baked. The second boy replied, "Well, it'll be mom baking cause last time we burned them up and filled the kitchen with smoke." The second boy asked, "Regular milk, chocolate milk or that almond stuff like on TV, or it is oat milk or goat milks?" The second boy said, "Or maybe you might like a cool juice box just to mix it up?" The first boy added, "Or we could sneak one of dad's whiskey stash, he'd never miss it, I hope." I told them I would be fine, except for the whiskey idea, with whatever they came up with Christmas Eve. The older boy said, "Cool, our dad said a good soldier is always prepared!"

A boy, 6, visited Santa at a military base recreation hall. He was looking down at the floor, shuffled his feet back and forth, finally looked up and said, "I cannot tell a lie, I screwed up all year long." Santa thanked the boy for his honesty. The little guy looked up again and replied, "Oh, it's not that, my sister wrote you a letter 'bout me, so I figured you already knew all the bad stuff!"

A boy, 7, came to see Santa and asked if he got a military jet escort on Christmas Eve. The boy was with his father who was a pilot Santa recognized from a year earlier. "Well, son, the military is on alert and ready to scramble at a moment's notice," I replied. Actually, I was pretty impressed at my own answer, but, then again, I impress easily! "Oh, thank heavens, cause with those glasses and all that hair and stuff, plus you gotta' be like a hundred, right," he replied. His dad roared with laughter and patted his son on the head. He said, "Don't you worry son, we always got Santa's six." His son seemed satisfied with that. A hundred, really???

A boy, 7, stopped to see Santa at his base holiday party. He stood right in front of me, folded his arms in front of his chest and said, "Dad's over in Hawaii supposedly for 'training.' I'm not buying it, I think he's on vacation without me," he added. Before I could get a word in, the boy added, "So, my wish is that you get him stationed next time near Disneyland or Disneyworld."

A little girl came to see Santa at a west coast military base and said, "I made this card and another picture for my daddy, he's in Japan." I told her both were beautiful, and her dad would love them. "Is it out of your way to deliver them to him," she asked. I told her I would be happy to and tell her dad how much she loved and missed him. She clapped her hands in glee and replied, "You're the bestest Santa never!"

A little boy had a very perplexed look on his face as he came up to Santa at a base children's holiday party. Santa asked what was on his mind, always a very risky idea! Sorry, had to add that. The boy looked up and said, "Do rockets have feet?" I asked him to explain a little further. He replied, "Well, I keep hearing bout missletoes and I'm so confused now."

A little girl visited Santa with her dad at a National Guard children's holiday party. She read her whole list and ended it with a final wish. "A brand-new uniform for my daddy," she said. He beamed at his little girl. I asked what kind of uniform she wanted for him. She replied, "Just a bigger one 'cause the one he has now won't button by his belly." I guess I should have stopped at the first answer.

A boy, 5, was with his dad at a military base children's Christmas party. The little guy was very talkative. I asked him what he'd like to be when he grew up. He replied, "A Marine, just like my daddy." Dad beamed, then his son added, "I like their hats!"

A girl, 6, told Santa that her daddy was in the Air Force. "He flies big, big planes," she said. I asked where he flies the planes. She replied, "In the air, silly!" I guess I'll never learn.

A boy, 6, visited with Santa at a base holiday party. He was with his mom. He told Santa that his daddy flew "Airplanes on a ship in the ocean." I asked him if he knew what kind of plane it was. He replied, "The kind that don't fall off the end of the ship when it lands." Mom roared at that one. She said she couldn't wait to share that with her husband and his fellow pilots.

CHAPTER 12

Children's Center Parties

Everywhere children gather for Christmas holiday parties: Boys & Girls Clubs, community centers, schools, churches, housing facilities, police, fire and sheriff's department halls, and everything in between are a huge part of the season. Visiting with several dozen or several hundred children plus their parents, grandparents and other family members is such fun. Every time I think I've literally heard it all, some child tops it. I'm continually in awe and amazement at these little characters and their minds in action. There's something about this wonderful, magical season that I can't explain. It just is Christmas! Children often come to these events decked out in what my generation referred to as their "Sunday best." Party dresses, colorful sweaters, shirts with bow ties, freshly pressed pants, newly polished shoes, and brand-new outfits are on display. One of my absolute favorite things over the years is doing annual Santa visits at the same locations. I treasure observing kids growing up at Christmas time. At some locations, I've known kids from holding them as a baby for their first Christmas all the way through the doubting age! At these events I know who everyone is and what family they belong to. I enjoy the friendly banter and back and forth between kids. I also truly enjoy watching older kids introduce their younger brothers and sisters to Santa and showing them how to be part of the whole experience. Being visited by entire families, encompassing several generations, is particularly joyful and rewarding. I love observing grandparents, great grandparents, parents, and the rest of the family members building holiday memories together with Santa. One absolutely amazing blessing that comes with being Santa is being part of a little child's first Christmas. Imagine the feeling of holding a months or even weeks old infant in your arms and having them look up at you for their first Christmas photo. The baby doesn't know, of course, what's going on, but the photos will be treasured by their family for many years.

A little boy came to see Santa at his local Boys and Girls Club. He had a somewhat perplexed look on his face and held a piece of paper. He said, "This is my first time, and so, my older brother told me to bring my laundry list." I smiled because I had heard this before and knew what was coming. "I don't know why you want to know about my socks and t-shirts and stuff, but here you goes," he said. I let him go on for a while, then said, "It's OK young man, like you said, you're new at this." I added, "What your brother meant was a list of presents you'd like for Christmas." The boy got all red in the face and replied, "I shoulda' known 'cause he's such a goofball, geez!"

A girl, 7, visited Santa and said, "I wasn't real impressed with what you brought last year, just saying!"

A little boy came to see Santa at the local Boys and Girls Club Christmas party. He stood in front of Santa with his hands in his pockets, a sheepish look on his face and teetered back and forth.

Finally, he looked up and blurted out, "I must confess my sins, I'm trouble."

A boy, 8, stopped to see Santa at a Christmas party in the town square. He asked, "Have you ever cheated on Mrs. Claus?" That was a first for me. I told him no, Santa was very loyal. I asked him where the question came from. He replied, "Well, I have a girlfriend, but there's a new girl at our school and she's a real hottie." He continued, "So, I thought, you know, if you did it, well, I could probably get away with it."

A girl, 7, was standing in line to visit Santa and kept shaking her head back and forth. When her time came, she blurted out, "How do you deal with all these kids crying and yelling. I find it all very annoying." I told her that children all go through stages of growing up and this was all part of it. She looked stunned and said, "Really, well, it's enough to make me become a nun!"

Twins, brother and sister, 6, visited with Santa and had worried looks on their faces. The girl talked first and said, "What's it means gift of gab?" I told them it meant people who like to talk a lot. They looked at each other and the girl whispered in her brother's ear. He hesitated and she said, "Ask him." The boy looked up and said, "If we got that, does it mean we get less other gifts for Christmas?"

A little boy came to see Santa and asked, "Do you think the Easter Bunnies' for reals?" Santa asked the boy what he thought. "Well, he's kinda big for a rabbit, you're just fat like Santa's 'posed to be," he replied. I probably should not have asked...

Two brothers, 6 and 7, visited with Santa at a Boys and Girls Club holiday party. The older boy asked Santa, "So you know what all us kids are doing all over the world all the time?" I replied yes, it was Santa magic. He continued, "So, like Batman, Superman, Spiderman and Aquaman all rolled into like one?" I smiled and said, "I guess you could say that young man." His eyes opened very wide, his jaw dropped, and he said to his brother, "Dude, you better tell him the whole truth 'cause he's got superpowers!"

A girl, 8, was visibly upset as she waited in Santa's line, folding her arms in front of her chest, and shifting her weight back and forth, back, and forth from one leg to the other. When she got to see Santa she asked, "Did you know that babies just sleep, cry and poop?" I just smiled since she was already speaking again. "We got one of those since I saw you last and it's really, really annoying, actually gross."

A little boy, 6, came to see Santa at his town's annual Christmas fair. He leaned in close to Santa's ear and said, "I hope this is really worth it, cause I had to take a bath before I came. And it wasn't even my time of the week yet, "he added.

A little boy came up the steps at his school Christmas pageant party and blurted out, "Can I like meet you halfway on all this be good stuff. Seems like I'm doing all the heavy liftin' you know!"

A girl, 5, asked Santa if "You still are eatin' cookies or do I leave you a plate of that glute stuff?"

"My teacher says I'm impossible," said a little boy to Santa at a church children's Christmas party. He added, "You think I'm gonna' get a' A?"

A boy, 7, told Santa, "My dad's a real rocket scientist, so I'm gonna' have him help me design you a cool, new sleigh with power boosters, twin rocket engines and other awesome stuff to speed things up." He was so excited that he could hardly contain himself. "I'll send you some preliminary drawings, OK," he added. I told him great, just not sure how Rudolph and the other reindeer will adjust!!!

A girl, 8, came to see Santa at her local church holiday festival. She had her mobile notebook, so I knew I was in for some serious questions. "Do you have an annual budget just for me or is it per family," she asked? "It will help me better prepare my request list," she added.

A little boy stopped to see Santa and said, "Mommy said I got to be good or there's serous 'continentsees."

A girl, 8, came to see Santa at her Boys and Girls Club and said she had a great efficiency idea. "I think I'll set up the nanny camera so I can record things and see what takes so long," she said. "We can analyze it and come up with some time saving ideas," she added.

A little boy talked with Santa about what he wanted to be when he grew up. "I want to be just like my daddy, he's a bachelor!" Not exactly sure how that works.

A boy, 7, visited Santa and held out his cellphone. "How bout you text me when you're done at our house, so I don't have to wait till Christmas morning," he said. Ah, yes, the creative mind at work!

A little boy and girl whispered to Santa, "Guess what, we think our Elf on the Shelf is a double agent!"

A boy, 7, told Santa, "If you need help eating all the cookies you get, I'm your man." He added, "Especially on our block 'cause lots of the mom's are good cooks." He continued, "I know 'cause at our school bake sale I use up all my allowance."

A little boy's Christmas wish list started with, "Change the eat all your veggies thing to eat extra dessert!"

A girl, 6, asked Santa, "Are you baby Jesus' daddy?" I explained the best I could about the true meaning of Christmas. She looked up at me, smiled and replied, "I still bet you'd be a good daddy."

A little girl stopped to see Santa for the first time at her local town hall Christmas party, stopped in her tracks, eyes wide open. She blurted out, "It ain't Halloween, what's the deal!"

A boy, 5, came to visit Santa and said, "I bet it's hot in there, huh?" I said yes, it did get quite warm sometimes. He smiled and said, "Next time just wear your PJ's." I like his thinking.

A girl, 4, was smiling as she came up the steps to the stage at a civic center children's Christmas party. She asked to sit on Santa's lap. She got settled in and smiled. She looked up and said, "I'm a mess waitin' ta' happen, the end."

A little boy, 5, asked Santa, "Is it OK to take money out a' the collection plate at church if you're short a' cash?"

A little girl told Santa she had a special secret. Santa asked her to lean in close to his ear so she could tell him. The girl did and said, "Mommy said not to tell you she's 44 and going downhill fast."

A boy, 6, told Santa he had a poem to tell him. Santa said he could not wait to hear it. "Well, roses are red, violets are blue and they're not my flowers 'cause I picked 'em from my neighbor's yard." That was a different version for sure!

A girl told Santa that she stopped calling her little brother by his first name. I asked her what she called him now. She replied, "By his new initials, P.U."

CHAPTER 13

Fire Shelters

A fire shelter worker once told me the next time I drove home and turned the corner into my neighborhood, picture absolutely nothing there. That very vivid image has been etched in my mind for many years. Everything you take for granted, all your treasures, all your keepsakes... gone. Temporary housing shelters, school gymnasiums, church halls, wherever fire victims gather after a horrific event are the very places Santa needs to be. Fires ravage our communities all year long but often especially during the holiday months. Santa needs to bring words of encouragement, hope, kindness, unity, caring and good cheer to these families plus to the first responders and relief workers that assist them. Often the visits from Santa are just to bring some sense of normalcy to a potentially hopeless time. Following these tragic fires, comes planning, rebuilding, a renewed sense of community, personal resolve, and partnerships. Santa's cap off to the Red Cross, National Guard, firefighting personnel, police/sheriffs/state patrol, EMT's and all shelter staff and volunteers. Blessings to all of you, and please keep pushing forward!

A little boy, 6, was at a wildfire temporary housing shelter and proclaimed to Santa, "Well, there's one of them silver mining things to all this, I don't have to turn in my homework!"

A girl, 7, told Santa sadly that all his special snickerdoodle cookies she had made with her mom were lost in their apartment fire. Santa told the girl that it was OK, he would have plenty of cookies at other houses. She smiled and added, "You might want to go easy on them 'cause you really are getting fat you know." So, one hundred years old, too fat… doesn't Santa get a break now and again too!

A little boy was all excited to talk to Santa. He leaned in close and said, "I gots a secret, wanna' know what it is?" Santa smiled and said sure. The boy whispered, "I'm gonna' be a uncle next month." Santa asked who was having a baby. The boy replied, "my brother, he got married last week." Best to leave that one alone.

A girl, 6, told Santa she learned something new at school after lots of practice. Her mom beamed until her daughter added, "How to whisper in class without moving my lips."

A boy, 6, told Santa that he had lost everything in a fire at his house. "I got nothing now," he said sadly. I pointed to his family, mom, dad, a brother, and sister. "You didn't lose everything young man," said Santa. The boy looked at his family, stared at the ground, then finally said, "Yea, you're right, I guess that's why you're Santa, huh?"

A boy, 7, told Santa his top wish was to get married at Christmas. Santa asked him who was going to be the lucky bride. Without hesitating, the boy replied, "Not sure she'd be so lucky, look at me." He was a bit of a mess with wrinkled shirt, scuffed shoes, uncombed hair, and untied shoelaces. Santa suggested he could be a better catch if he cleaned up a bit. The boy replied, "Sounds like a lot a work just to be caught." Santa smiled as the boy added, "I'll just stay a bachelor and play the field."

A little boy, 4, visited with Santa at a temporary housing hall. He stood in front of Santa and threw up his arms over his head and said, "All my stuffs gone." Santa tried to console him and replied, "You can always get new stuff son." The boy replied, "But I like my stuff." Santa smiled and said he got it and would try to bring him "some cool new stuff" at Christmas. The little guy perked up and said, "Oh, for reals, forget about the old stuffs then."

A girl talked with Santa about her experience so far in the shelter. "I don't get it, they gave me a plastic cap when I take a shower," she said. Santa smiled as she continued, "What's the point of a shower if I'm gonna' cover everything up?"

A little girl was all excited to see Santa and could hardly wait to talk to him. She stood in front of Santa and gleefully said, "Santa, Santa, do you know why all the kids love Frosty the snowman?" I knew where this was headed but let her finish anyway! "'Cause he's so cool, get it, he's made a' snow and cool," she added.

A boy, 6, told Santa he wanted a new toy he heard his mom and dad talk about all the time. Santa asked him to go on. The little guy said, "I got lots a balls like a baseball and football and all that." Santa smiled and asked him what kind of new ball he would like for Christmas. The boy replied, "I guess it's something special 'cause it's called a hi-ball, must go way up in the air," he replied.

A little girl asked Santa why the Christmas tree went to the beauty shop. Before I could respond, she laughed and said, "'Cause it needed a trim, silly!"

A little boy visited with Santa at a shelter and said he 'mezmeri-seed" his Christmas wish list. I asked him what all was on his list.

He looked up in the air, down at the ground and back up in the air. He raised his arms above his head and said, "I forgot."

A girl talked with Santa and said she had a secret. She leaned in close and said, "Mommy says she's 30, but I think she's counting backwards."

A little boy was giggling and could hardly stop long enough to tell Santa his favorite Christmas joke. He finally said, "Santa, do you know what snowmen eat for breakfast?" Ah, yes, here it comes. "Snowflakes, that's what," he added as he started laughing with a few snorts as well.

A girl, 7, said to Santa, "I'm really sad, everything is gone now. What will we do, where will we live?" I told her even though it looked bad right now, things would get better every day and soon she and her family would have a new place to live. She looked at me and said, "Promise?" I said yes, promise. She gave me a big hug and replied, "When we get a new house, I'll leave lots of extra cookies for you next Christmas, OK?" Deal!

A boy, 7, told Santa he had learned all about Joan of Arc in school. "I think she's married to Noah," he added.

A girl told Santa she had a funny joke for him. Santa smiled and asked her to tell him. She replied, "What do you get when you cross a' apple and a Christmas tree?" Before I could ask, she added, "A pineapple, get it!"

A little boy told Santa he had a question for him. I asked him to go ahead and ask when he was ready. "You know how I can get to be a judge?" I had not heard that one before, so I asked him why he was interested in being a judge. He replied, "I just like saying, you're guilty, go to jail!"

A girl, 6, told Santa that her only Christmas wish was to be forty. Santa asked her why she wanted to be that age. The girl replied, "Mommy says life starts at 40, so I want to skip to that real fast."

A boy, 6, told Santa at a temporary housing center that he was very confused. I asked him to explain. The boy replied, "Well, Pastor Eric says that God made me." I asked him to go on. The boy added, "Well, then why am I always in trouble?" I think we will leave that to Pastor Eric to answer!

A little boy at a fire shelter told Santa that he did not like it when relatives came to visit at their house. Santa asked why and he replied, "'Cause then I gotta' clean my room." Before I could reply, he said, "Guess I'm off the hook now, huh?"

A boy, 5, told Santa there was only one good thing so far about staying at the fire victim shelter. Santa asked him what it was. Without blinking the boy replied, "Not so many baths!"

A little girl told Santa she wanted to go to a new school when she left the shelter with her family. Santa asked her which one. She replied, "The North Pole school, so Mrs. Claus can be my teacher." Apple polisher!

A boy, 6, told Santa that he had decided that he wanted to be a magician when he grew up. Santa asked him what tricks he would do. The boy thought for a while and finally replied, "I say aba-daba-do and pull a' elefunk out of a hat." Actually, I would like to see that myself.

A little girl told Santa she would like to get a watch for her Christmas gift. Santa asked if she could tell time. The girl replied, "Sure." I asked her what time it was right then, and she replied, "It's nighttime, silly."

A little boy told me he had learned a new prayer at the shelter his family was staying at. "Wanna' hear it," he asked? I told him of course. "Now I lay me down to eat, hope there's good stuff to eat, I think that's how it goes," he replied. Close!

A girl visited with Santa and whispered that she learned a new joke. Santa asked her to tell him. "OK, what's Christmas trees' favorite candy," she asked? I told her that I did not know. She replied, "It's ornamints, that's what."

A boy, 9, seemed overly sad and his parents asked that I take him aside to talk. He sat next to me and said, "Why do we have to be here, why did this happen to us?" I told him that wildfires are exactly as the name is, wild, and cannot be predicted. He continued, "But, why us, we're good people?" I told him there would always be sad things that happen to good people in his lifetime, but never to give up, never look back, and keep moving forward. He asked, "Is God mad at us, did we do something wrong?" I assured him that God always loves him and his family, they did nothing wrong, fires just happen. "Soon you'll have a fresh, new start in your young life plus you have your whole life ahead of you," I said. He looked me square in the eyes and said, "Bet you hear a lot of real sad stories from all the families, huh?" I told him yes, but the bright thing was that all the families at the temporary housing hall, especially his family, were all safe and healthy. That was the important thing. He looked down and then back at me and replied, "I never thought about that part, guess I was just being selfish." I told him it was OK, he had never dealt with anything like this, so he had nothing to compare it to. We got up, went back to where his family was sitting. He asked them to "bring it in" and gave them all a big bear hug.

CHAPTER 14

Young Love

I wish I had kept track of how many times Santa has been asked to "marriaged" little couples. Young love is one of the sweetest and most precious things that Santa gets to observe. I'm not sure why Santa ends up being the first choice of these lovebirds to marry them, but it happens often. Two kids, holding hands, standing in front of Santa sharing their hopes and dreams is just too cute. These little couples are also hilarious, especially because they are often so very, very serious! Typically, they have the whole process backwards and mispronounced, but that's half the fun of it. It's also important for Santa not to laugh during the conversation due to how committed the kids are. You never know the full story when they stop by. Boys typically are looking to marry so that another boy doesn't steal their wife to be. Girls typically are looking to play house or start a family. Children pick up so much today from television, movies, the internet, videos, music, classmates, and siblings. Often, they are way ahead of even Santa on what's what. Why the clergy is not asked more often by these kids to marry them has always surprised me. I fondly remember asking a little boy why he and his future bride didn't ask their church minister to do the honors.

Without missing a beat, he replied, "Oh, no, he don't do that, he just hands out treats to adults at the altar."

Two girls, both 7, and best friends, came to visit Santa at a local Boys and Girls Club. They stood in front of him, gave him the once over, up, and down and side to side. Finally, one said to the other, "You're right, Mrs. Claus could've done better, just saying." Ouch!!!

A little boy and girl stopped to see Santa and very excitedly blurted out together, "We're getting weddinged." They continued, "We're gonna' have pudding cups, juice boxes with straws and lots and lots of cake and ice cream!"

A little girl told Santa that she was going to get "marriaged" soon. I asked her what her husband to be had to be like. "Oh, he can't be single, he has to be a bachelor," she replied. I would have scratched my head, but I had that Santa cap on.

A girl, 5, came to see Santa and had a very frantic look on her face. She said, "It's over with Quinn!" I asked her what had happened. She raised her arms above her head and said, "So, he flushed my goldfish and turtle down the toilet, that's what." Yes, that pretty much would end any serious relationship.

A little boy asked Santa if he knew a lot about music. Santa replied that he did and asked how he could help. The boy said he was planning to get married, and his grandpa told him to get a cigar band. I could tell this one was going to take a while.

A girl, 7, told Santa that she had three wishes on her Christmas list. "A Lexus, a rich husband and triplets," she announced. Santa asked her about the interesting list of wishes. She calmly replied, "Yes, I just want to get it all over with at once." Sounds like she has a plan.

A boy, 7, came to see Santa at his church holiday party. He had a very serious look on his face, hands in his pockets and was teetering back and forth. Finally, he asked, "How did you know Mrs. Claus was the one?" I told him we both looked into each other's eyes, and we just knew. He looked confused and replied, "What's her eyes got to do with it, was she a hottie or not back then???"

A little girl stopped to see Santa and asked, "You know any good married men?" I asked what she meant. "Oh, I'm ready to get married, so I figure one of that kind of man has 'sperience."

A girl, 7, replied when Santa asked what she wanted for Christmas. "The three m's, money, makeup and a man, "she replied without hesitation.

A boy, 6, visited Santa at his local fire department children's holiday party. He leaned in close and whispered, "Know any good safe houses?" Before I could respond, he added, "This girl at school has the hots for me and she's kinda' a stalker."

A girl, 6, told Santa that she had decided that it was time to start dating. Santa asked her what the most important thing was to find out about her intended future boyfriend. "His text number," she replied.

A girl visited Santa and declared that she was going to get married. I asked if she had someone in mind. She replied," Yes, but he has to stay a bachelor 'cause they got more money than married men."

A little boy came to see Santa at his church holiday party. He leaned in close and whispered, "I'm thinking 'bout getting married." I smiled as he added, "Do you know if you need to take an extra bath that week for that?"

A little girl, 7, stopped to see Santa and told him that she had finally found her man. Santa asked her how she knew he was the one. "Well, first he said yuk, then he said he couldn't stand me. Then he said he never wanted to see me ever again, so, I figured he was just playing hard to get you know," she replied.

A boy told Santa that he had decided it was time to get married. I asked him his age and he replied, "Six and three quarters." I then asked if he had anyone in mind. He said, "Yes, my mom, 'cause she knows all the tricks!" I decided to leave it there.

A little girl blurted out, "The 'gagements off." Santa asked her what happened. She replied, "Well, we're having ice cream sundaes at the wedding, and he wants colored sprinkles and I want just chocolate ones."

A boy, 6, told Santa that he was getting married soon. I asked him if he had his wife picked out. He replied, "Yup." I inquired if he had found a house to live in and he said, "Yup." I asked where they would go on a honeymoon. "Disneyland, of course!" Should have seen that one coming.

A little girl told Santa she was going to get married to a Prince. I asked if that made her a Princess. She replied, "Oh, yes, of course." I asked what she would do as a new Princess. "Sit on my gold throne and boss the prince," she replied.

In a comparable situation, a little girl told Santa her favorite bedtime story was Sleeping Beauty. Santa asked what she liked the most about the story. She replied, "Having the prince by your bedside so he can kiss you."

A boy, 7, asked Santa if he had spotted any "hotties" so far at the Boys and Girls Club Christmas party. I asked him if that meant he needed some help with the ladies. The boy replied, "Oh, no, I'm a really smooth talker. I'm just looking for a wingman!" I've been asked to fill a lot of roles as Santa, but that was a first.

A girl, 6, visited with Santa at her local Boys and Girls Club holiday party. She was sad as she told him that she had to break off the engagement with her future husband Russell. Santa inquired why. "Well, he farts and picks his nose, that's why," she replied. Yes, that's a deal breaker!

A little girl and boy came to see Santa and announced that they had decided to be married. I asked them what they would like to be when they grew up. They both looked at each other and the boy replied, "Oh, nothin, ' we just wanna' stay kids!"

A little boy told Santa that he was now married. Santa asked how the marriage was going. The boy replied, "So far, so good." Santa asked what the boy would do if the marriage was not working out so well. The boy replied, "We'd play hide and seek, and I wouldn't look for her!"

A little girl told Santa that she was going to get married. "I'm going to be a be a mother, the kind that has babies."

A girl, 5, told Santa that she was having second thoughts about her husband to be, Philip. I asked what the problem was. She replied, "He drinks his juice box too fast and burps, plus he colors outside the lines all the time."

A very frantic little boy marched up to Santa and blurted out, "I think my girlfriend is part puppy." Santa inquired further and the boy replied, "Well, she just licked me!"

A little boy and girl stopped to see Santa and told him they would like to get married right then. I asked if they had thought things through if they really knew enough about each other. The boy leaned in close and said, "Well, she told me not to tell you that she's kinda sloppy." The girl overheard him, stamped her foot, put her hands on her hips and declared, "Forget it, I'm leavin' you at the alter," and marched off.

A little boy told Santa he had a very important question about getting married. I prepared myself for what was to come. He leaned in close and asked, "When you say I do, is that for like everything, forever, really, geez!"

A girl, 6, visited Santa and said she had picked out her future husband. I asked how she knew that he was the one. She replied that he was very intelligent and knew all 'bout the law. I inquired further and she replied, "Well, I told him I want to be with him forever, so he said he was gonna' take out 'straining orders."

A little boy and girl came to see Santa holding hands. The boy went first and said, "Do you do the I do stuff?" The girl brushed him aside and said, "Men, what's a girl to do?" She added, "He means can you 'marriage' us right away?" Santa asked if they were ready to take the leap. The boy looked puzzled and said, "I do that lots at recess." The girl jumped in again and said, "I got this, don't worry 'bout him, he's the husband, he doesn't have a say." And so, it begins!

A little girl stopped to see Santa at her local Boys and Girls Club and announced that she was going to be "wedded" very soon. I asked her what the most important thing her new husband would have to do after the wedding. Without thinking, she replied, "Give me all his money."

A little boy marched up the steps to the stage at a school Christmas party to visit with Santa. He looked very seriously at Santa and said, "Do you think I'm old enough to get married?" I asked him his age and he replied, "Well, I'm like five and three quarters and a half."

A little girl and her husband to be came to see Santa and said they were now married and going on their honeymoon. I asked them where they were going. The girl replied, "To the Grand Canyon." I then asked what they would do when they got there.

The little boy put his hands up around his mouth and said, "Yell and holler into it real loud."

A boy and girl, both 7, stopped to see Santa at their local Boys and Girls Club. The boy said, "We decided to skip right to nine years old." I asked why and the girl replied, "'Cause his buddy said when you turn eight, you learn about the birds and the bees, and we already know all that." I decided to leave that one alone.

CHAPTER 15

Siblings

Being the middle brother in a family of three boys, I do understand sibling rivalry. Brothers and sisters, older and younger, it's lots of fun to watch and be part of. Santa, of course, has a front row seat as all of this plays out. Telling on each other is the number one goal especially for brothers and sisters. The best situation is where siblings are separated from each other in the line to see Santa. After the first one to get to Santa is finished telling all, I can often tell who they were giving up when the target makes it to the front of the line. These visits are among my favorites. Of course, Santa has to keep a straight face and show sincere interest as siblings tell on each other or "rat" each other out as boys say. Girls, in particular, are very serious about the misdeeds of their brothers, older and younger. Lots of eye rolling and hands on the hips. Boys often just shrug their shoulders and smile when accused of alleged horrible misconduct. If their sisters get to Santa first, boys will often arrive arms folded in front of their chests ready for the inquisition to begin. Brotherly competition is fun to observe as well. Ah, yes, it's all coming back to me now!

A boy, 7, came to see Santa with his wish list. At the very top was $100 million. Santa was surprised at the wish and asked for more information. The boy said he had seen on the TV news that people could buy trips to space. "I want to send my sister up there and keep her there until the money runs out," he said.

A girl, 7, visited with Santa and asked if he had a return or trade program for Christmas gifts. I inquired further and she said, "Well, we got a new baby last Christmas and all he does is poop and cry." Santa said that all little babies do that, and he would grow out of it in time. "Hmmm, well, how 'bout we give him back to you for now, then when he's grown out of that, we'll take him back," she said.

A girl, 8, seemed very upset when she made it through the line to talk to Santa. She finally got her chance and asked, very seriously, "Do you have kids?" I told her no, Mrs. Claus and I had all the elves to look after. She replied, "Well, I've got two younger brothers that you can adopt, and take both of them home with you today." She then pulled out a $20 bill and added, "There's more where this came from, just saying!"

A boy, 6, stopped to see Santa and said he had a real problem with his baby brother. I asked him for more information. He said the family recently went to Disney World. "My brother kept crapping in his diapers, and it slowed us down." He added, "I missed lots of rides 'cause of him." Santa assured him it would pass in time. The boy replied, "Well, I think I deserve another trip there for Christmas just to make up for stuff I missed out on."

A girl, 7, asked Santa if he had any job openings for elves. I thought she was going to say she would like to apply. Instead, she said, "The best Christmas present you can give me this year is to take Mason, my older brother, back to the North Pole with you and make him useful for something." She added, "Looking at all those elves, I think he'll fit right in."

Santa asked a little boy if he had been a good boy all year long. The boy looked up and replied, "I been a good loser." Santa asked him what he meant by that. Without blinking, the little guy replied, "I got four older brothers, so I'm good at losing."

A little girl told Santa she had a secret about her baby brother. Santa leaned down close, and the girl whispered, "He sneezed, and it came out the other end too!"

A boy, 6, came to visit Santa at his local church Christmas pageant and asked, "Is it true that Mars is really red?" Santa said yes it was. The boy replied, "How about we rocket up my sister there just to make sure!"

A little boy visited Santa and told him he had a big brother and a big sister. Santa asked if his brother was good to him. The boy hesitated, looked down at the ground and shifted from one leg to the other. He finally looked up and replied, "Can't quite say 'cause he's next in line there."

A girl, 5, told Santa that she has a new little baby brother. Santa asked her if her brother was here at the Christmas party that day. "Oh no, he's too lazy to walk yet," she replied.

Twin brothers, 5, came to see Santa at a police reserve children's holiday party. When Santa asked the boys if they had been good the past year, one brother pointed to the other and blurted out, "He did it!"

A boy, 7, told Santa that his number one wish for Christmas was for a way to be invisible. Santa inquired further and the boy replied, "'Cause when my mom gets mad at me, and she does that lots, I like to disappear."

A little boy told Santa that he really did not like school so far. Santa asked him why. He replied, "My brother walks me there so I can't step in the puddles." Santa said that did not sound so bad, that way his shoes stayed dry. The boy raised his arms above his head and said, "Yea, but I can't read yet, I can't write yet, plus my teacher won't let me talk. Why go?"

A girl, 6, came to see Santa with her younger brother, 5. When Santa asked if she had any bad habits, she pointed to her brother and replied, "Him!"

A little boy was all proud when he marched up the steps to the stage at his school holiday party. He announced to Santa, "Guess what, I can write now!" Santa said that was quite the accomplishment. "What do you write" asked Santa? The boy looked all flustered and said, "Don't know, I don't read so good."

A little girl visited Santa and told him she had a new baby brother. Santa asked how it was going so far. The girl replied, "Oh, it's so annoying, he cries all the time, glad I was so perfect."

A boy, 7, told Santa that he could not wait to get to high school to take biology. Santa told him it was a very good goal to be interested in all the sciences. The boy replied, "Nope, just biology." Santa asked him to explain. "Well, I hear you get to dissect bugs, so the first one I'll work on is my sister," he explained. I guess I should have known that was far too easy.

A girl, 7, complained to Santa that "My little brother is a real stinker." Santa asked if he misbehaves. The girl replied, "Yea, that too, but mostly he just stinks!"

A little boy told Santa that he had been a very good little boy all year long. Santa smiled and asked him for an example. The boy replied, "Well, I got 4 sisters and a mommy, and I never leave the toilet seat up."

A boy, 5, came to see Santa at his local Boys and Girls Club Christmas party. He told Santa he only had one wish for this year. Santa asked him what he wanted. The boy replied, "I just want to be a little mouse." Intrigued, I asked him to explain. "'Cause when my big brother is after me, I go into my little hole, that's why."

A girl, 6, stopped to see Santa and told him that her mommy was expecting and was going to have twins. Santa replied that it sounded very exciting. The girl replied, "Yep, I think it was one of those 2 for 1 sales."

A little boy visited Santa with his Christmas wish list and at the very top was weasel spray. Santa was intrigued and asked for further information. The boy looked up and said, "My older brother's a real weasel so I gotta' take him out!"

A boy, 5, was all out of breath when he got to the church Christmas pageant. He asked Santa if he had an extra box of corks on the sleigh. I thought I knew where this was going, but I had to ask him to explain. "My older sister keeps telling me to put a cork in it so I think I'll probably need lots of them," he replied.

A little girl had a very serious look on her face as she approached Santa. She leaned close to Santa's ear and said, "I needs bobyguards." I asked her what was going on. She replied, "I got lots of brothers and sisters and I'm a squealer."

A boy, 5, told Santa he was really tired of being called a blabbermouth. Santa asked him who was saying that about him. "Everybody," he replied. Santa asked him why he thought people would say that. Without blinking, he replied, "'Cause I blab!"

A little boy asked Santa if he knew what "an ugly stick was." I told him that I think I had heard about that. "Why would you ask," I said. "'Cause I think my sister got hit with it lots and lots of times," he replied.

Santa asked a little boy if he had any brothers or sisters. The little guy looked up and replied, "Nope, I'm still single."

A girl, 6, visited Santa and asked if she could trade in her younger brother. Santa asked her why she wanted to do that. She replied, "'Cause he's un-normal, that's why." I asked her what kinds of things he did that were "un-normal." "Everything," she replied. "Just yesterday, he fed a bag of microwave popcorn to my goldfish, and she died," she added. Santa asked her if she wanted a new goldfish then for Christmas. "Nope, just take back my brother and it's even, steven," she replied.

A boy, 7, seemed very concerned about seeing Santa at his local fire department children's holiday party. Waiting in line, he peered around the line numerous times as he got closer. Finally, it was his turn. "Man, I didn't know if you'd leave before I got up here," he said. I assured him that Santa would stay until everyone had made it through the line. "OK, cool, so, problem is my sister wrote you our family Christmas letter," he said. I asked why it was a problem. He replied, "She probably ratted me out, she's like that you know." I asked him what he had done during the year that would cause him to be concerned. As happens a lot at these moments, he looked back at the line and said, "Yea, you don't have enough time today, I'll write you a whole new letter defending me."

A girl, 7, visited Santa and asked, "You got any vacancies for elves?" Santa said that he and Mrs. Claus had all we needed for that Christmas season. She added, "How about feeding the reindeer or shoveling their poop?" I asked her to explain further. She just shook her head and said, "My two brothers are just useless, so I figured you might have something for them to do." Before I could respond she added, "How about you just take them in your sleigh and dump them off at the space station without a parachute!"

Two brothers, 4 and 6, came to talk with Santa. The younger boy said, "Do you know where back is?" Santa showed him where his front was and where his back was. The older brother said, "No, silly, we know that." I asked him to explain more. "Daddy and mommy said if we weren't better boys, they would send us back where we came from," he replied.

A boy, 7, came to see Santa with a very perplexed look on his face. "Can you find out if our family is some kinda' royalty and all that, he asked." Santa asked if he wanted an ancestry kit for Christmas. He replied, "No, that's OK, I'm trying to figure it out, first my older sister says she was a Princess, then a Queen and now a Diva, I'm lost!"

A little boy told Santa that he needed to confess sins. Santa asked him what he had done. The boy replied, "Well, I like to pick fights with my sister." Santa asked him why. The boy said, "'Cause she's smaller than me, duh!"

A special personal note of sibling rivalry. I have lived in thirteen cities in nine states in my lifetime. It's been hard enough for adults to keep track of me, so you can imagine what it would be like for kids. I'm not sure why children have trouble pronouncing the letter D early on, it just is. My oldest niece, Maureen, called me "Uncle Gon." She also asked, several times, "Where are you now?" I thought for a long time that my other niece and nephew, Janelle, and Keith, were also calling me that. Turns out they had actually named me "Uncle Gone." Each claims credit for that nickname, we'll probably never know for sure. When the three of us get together, the subject typically comes up, and the discussion goes on and on and on...

CHAPTER 16

Women's and Children's Shelters

Shelters for women and children seeking safety, security, relief, and counseling at temporary housing to regroup and rebuild are such blessings in life. Visits by Santa Claus during the holiday period can bring some good cheer, especially to the children. Due to the security requirements in many situations, Santa often does not know the location of the shelter until he's taken there by staff members. Santa is filled in by the staff in advance on each family to help understand their unique situation, what to say and how to respond. Listening is crucial because children especially are usually holding in feelings and emotions. Santa becomes that safe, welcoming adult to open up to. Between Thanksgiving and Christmas, too many families fall apart for numerous reasons. I have seen enough black eyes, split lips, broken bones, cigarette burns, slumped shoulders, and sad eyes to last more than a lifetime. Being able to give a child a few toys and treats at a time when they often have nothing but the proverbial clothes on their backs is a joy. This is where Santa needs to be perhaps more than anywhere else. Bringing a smile, a hug, a cheerful voice and words of hope, encouragement and kindness can go a long way to help heal physical and emotional wounds. Santa's cap off another time for the shelter staffs, first responders and social services workers who rescue, take people in, bind the bodies, ease the minds, and provide a safe place needed at this time of need in people's lives.

A little boy visited with Santa at a shelter. He was asked what he would like to be when he grew up. He answered, "Nothing." Santa was very concerned by his answer until the little guy added, "I don't want to grow up, I like being a kid!"

Santa asked a little girl what the first thing was she would do on Christmas morning. She thought for a few seconds and finally replied, "Wake up, I guess." I liked her thinking.

Twin brother and sister, 7, talked with Santa at a family shelter. The boy announced that he was "First in his class at school." His sister replied, "No you're not, not even close." He answered and said, "Yup, first out the door for recess and to go home!" Creative minds at work for sure.

Santa joined three families for dinner at a women and children's shelter. Santa asked a little boy what his favorite part of the turkey was. Without hesitating, the boy replied, "The part with meat on it."

A little boy told Santa that he only wanted one thing for Christmas. I asked him what his wish was. He replied, "Tons of money so I can buy a toy store." I asked him if he would let his brothers and sisters come to the store to pick out some Christmas toys. He thought about it and replied, "If they got a credit card, sure." A true businessman in training.

A three-year-old boy sat on Santa's knee and pulled his beard. He looked up at Santa and said, "Sorry, I's not 'sponsible for my actions."

A girl, 7, sat sadly on a window ledge at a women's and children's shelter. She looked out and tears started coming down her face. Santa stopped by and sat with her. Finally, she said, "I don't get it, why don't they love me?" I told her sometimes parents change because of things in their lives, but lots and lots of people loved her. She smiled a very weak smile and said, "Do you love me too?" I told her Santa would always love her and her life would get better with every day. "By Christmas sweetheart, you'll be outside playing again, going to school in the new year and having fun," I said. She put her head on my shoulder and said, "I believe you." Right then her aunt and uncle arrived from a city nearby, rushed up and gave her a huge hug. She looked at me, smiled, and said, "It's starting already Santa."

Santa asked a little boy what kinds of toys he would like to replace those he had lost in his house fire. The boy thought for a bit and replied, "Some dinosaurs, like prehistoric, you know, really, really old, like you!"

A little girl, 6, told Santa that her Christmas wish was to be twelve-years-old right away. He asked her why. She replied, "'Cause you got a bigger stomach for cake and ice cream, that's why, silly."

A little boy had a slight cold when Santa visited him at a shelter. Santa asked if he needed anything like cough drops or Kleenex. The boy replied, "Nope, I'm gonna' get honey, lemon and bour-bon like grandpa does." Nothing works as well as good old home remedies!

A girl, 6, asked Santa what it was like to meet the M & M's that she saw on a TV commercial. She repeated the lines from the commercial; "He's real," and "They're real." Santa laughed as the little girl added, "I like the yellow one best 'cause he's kinda' dumb like my brother."

Santa asked a little boy what his favorite song was. The boy replied, "Jesus Loves Me." I told him that was one of my favorite songs too. The boy replied, "Yea, I figure somebody's got to!"

A brother and sister talked with Santa at a women's and children's shelter. The girl said, "We can't leave you cookies and milk 'cause we got no home right now." Santa said it was ok, he gets lots and lots of cookies and milk all the time. The boy replied, "Cool, 'cause I'm kinda' a cookie thief anyways."

Santa asked a little boy what he would like to be when he grew up. The boy thought hard for a bit and finally replied, "Anything but a bird." Santa asked him to explain. The boy said, "Well, I ate a worm, and I didn't like it."

A little boy was doing his homework at a shelter when Santa stopped by to visit. Santa asked the boy what his Christmas wish was. The boy looked up and said, "Just one, can you show me how to get better grades, without cheating!" I think Mom took note of that one.

A little girl told Santa that she had a secret. He leaned down close, and she whispered, "I saw you last Christmas Eve." Santa was surprised as the girl added, "But you had your PJ's on and a beer."

Santa asked a boy, 7, what he would like to be when he grew older. The boy replied, "I want your job." Santa asked him to explain. Without hesitating the boy replied, "Well, you work one day a year, fly to cool places, the elves do the chores, and you eat all the cookies you want!" Hard to argue with that.

A little girl looked up at Santa, smiled and said, "Mr. Santa, can you fix my report card, pretty please!" Santa asked her what was on the report card that needed fixing. She replied, "The part that says I talk too much in class."

A little boy told Santa that the firefighters came and rescued him and his family when their apartment was on fire. He asked, "Could you let them slide down your north pole sometimes and then I can come too."

A little girl told Santa she had a secret. Santa asked what it was, and the girl replied, "Mommy told me the two magic words." I asked what the words were. She whispered, "Please and thank you." Good life lessons from mom early on.

A girl told Santa that she had decided she was going to be a mother when she grew up. Santa asked her how many children she wanted to have. Without blinking she replied, "Oh, none of those, kids are so disturbing." I had to go further and asked her what kind of husband she would like. She replied, "One that's not married." I guess she had it all planned out.

A little boy told Santa at a shelter that his only wish for Christmas was to get a puppy. "I need one so I can drop food off the table I don't like," he added. Quickly he added, "Course, right now, we don't have much a' that, so I'll wait a bit on the dog, ok?"

A boy was very concerned when he got to talk with Santa at a women's and children's shelter. "So, I wrote you a letter, but everything's changed now," he said. Santa asked him what he could do to help. The boy replied, "Well, I asked for your spare reindeer for our backyard and spare elves to make toys in our garage. But now I got nowhere for them." The boy looked down at the ground and got very quiet. Tears started flowing down his cheek. I put my arm around him and said I would text Mrs. Claus to set his letter aside until life got a little better for him. The boy looked up relieved. I told him our lives are like rollercoasters sometimes and he would be back on top in no time. He smiled and replied, "I love rollercoasters, just not the getting off part!"

A little boy came up to Santa and was beaming from ear to ear. Santa asked why he was so happy. He said, "We played a game yesterday and I won the big prize." Santa asked how he did so good at the game. The boy leaned in close to Santa's ear and replied, "'Cause I cheated!"

A girl, 6, told Santa that she was not sure she would be going back to school. Santa assured her that things would get better soon, and she could see all her friends at school again. The girl replied, "I'm not so sure, my teacher says I'm a class disrupter." Santa smiled and asked her if she knew the meaning of the word disrupter. The little girl said, "I think it means time out is coming." She added, "I spend a lot a time in the corner too." Santa asked the girl if she could try harder to be better in school. The girl thought for a bit and replied, "Nope, where's the fun in that?" Ok, I tried, I really did.

A little boy, 5, told Santa that his dog Lucy had just had puppies. He added, "I didn't even know she was married, just saying."

Three kids at a women's and children's shelter asked Santa if he would tell their mom some funny jokes. "She's really sad right now, please," said the oldest child. Santa took their mom aside and told her his top ten favorite kids' jokes. She laughed and laughed at all the corny jokes. Just then the kids came back over and the oldest said, "It's gonna' be OK mommy, Santa's got this."

CHAPTER 17

The Naughty List

Why is it that only boys are concerned about being on the naughty list? In all my years being Santa, I have yet to have one little girl worried about it. Kids are always more frantic about where they stand the closer it gets to Christmas. Panic sets in as the days on the December calendar are crossed off at home. It's also fun to visit with children whose parents have used the naughty or nice list as a bargaining tool for better behavior. The excuses, concerns, schemes, explanations, and offers are often priceless.

A boy, 7, came to see Santa at a military base children's holiday party. I asked him his name and age, then said, "Have you been a good boy this past year?" He looked at me, stared down at the floor, shifted from one foot to the other and finally replied, "Can we just skip that one for now and go right to my wish list for presents?" "PLEASE," he pleaded.

A little boy, 6, was at a Boys and Girls Club Christmas party, walked up to Santa, folded his arms across his chest, stood up very tall and announced, "I pleads the 5th!" "I don't know what it means, but it worked on a TV show I saw at home," he added.

A boy, 7, told Santa, "I really like Moses from the Bible." I asked him what he liked the most about him. "'Cause he's kinda' like me, breaks stuff, like those tablets," he replied. Not quite sure that is what I was expecting.

"Can you define good," said the little boy to Santa at his local sheriff's department children's Christmas party. He added, "I just wanna' see if I'm on the right tracks, you know."

A boy, 6, told Santa that he, "Had a tough year, things really got out of control with my sister, you know." Santa asked the little guy what all had happened. The boy looked behind him at the long line of children waiting to see Santa and replied, "I don't think you got enough time today."

A boy, 7, visited with Santa at his church recreation hall. When I asked him whether he had been a good guy all year, he replied, "I refuse to answer that without my lawyer present." He added, "Pretty cool, huh?"

Two twin brothers, 6, came to Santa at a fire department holiday party. They were all out of breath when they made it into the building. The spokesman of the two said, "We were thinking that since we get in trouble together most the time, that it should only count half for each of us." Santa was impressed by their creativity and told them that if they only got into half as much trouble, it would be even better. "What you think?" said the first boy. His brother replied, "Na, ' I like your first idea a lot better."

A boy, 8, stopped to see Santa at a military base children's holiday party. Santa asked him if he had been a good boy all year long. The boy stopped and thought for a bit. He looked over at his older brother who had brought him to the party. He thought a bit more and finally asked, "Do I need an attorney present?"

Santa asked a boy to tell him what one of the best things about him would be. The boy replied, "I'd say I'm dependable." Then he smiled and added, "You can pretty much depend on me to always get in some kinda' trouble." I knew it was coming, but that one never gets old!

A boy, 7, asked Santa if a person is on the naughty list forever once they get on it. Before I could answer, he added, "'Cause I think I'm probably a lifer!"

A boy 7, asked Santa, "Before we start, can you explain a little naughty, kinda' naughty and really, really naughty for me."

A little boy, 6, came to see Santa at his local school holiday party. He was a little nervous, shuffled from one foot to the other, and looked down at the floor. Finally, he looked up and said, "How much naughty stuff gets you kicked off the nice list?"

A boy, 7, said to Santa, "My older brother is in high school, and he got his records sealed, can I work something out like that with you too?" All I could do is smile. "Yea, I figured," he replied.

A little boy, 6, visited with Santa at a National Guard children's holiday party. He had waited a long time in line. He marched up the steps of the stage and stood right in front of Santa. "Not sure how's to say this, but how much stuff you do counts on being naughty or nice." He continued, "Like, you know, gross stuff to your sister and all that."

A boy, 8, pointed over his head and said, "It's like I got this black cloud on top of me all the time Santa." I told him we all had rough days when it seemed everything was going wrong. "Well, let me tell you, this has been going on since I was born from what I can remember," he replied. "On a scale of 1 to 10, my life is like a minus 6," he added. I told him that perhaps next year would be better. He replied, "I sure hope so, or I'll never see another Christmas gift ever again!"

A boy, 7, visited Santa and said, "So, my brother is like Mr. perfect, Mr. goody two shoes and stuff." I smiled and let him go on. "So, how 'bout we take some of my bad stuff and drop it onto his record and that way I get some relief, plus it won't really hurt his deal, right?" That was a new way to look at it for sure.

A boy, 6, came to a police department children's holiday party. He had his cell phone with him. He held it out to me and said, "Can I get a text from you on here when I'm gonna' move from the nice to naughty list?" He added, "That way I can make some moves, you know."

Two brothers, 6 and 7, came up to Santa together. The first one said, "Why do mommy and daddy make it so hard to be on the nice list?" The second one added, "Yea, maybe if you talk to them, they'll cut us slack and stuff."

A boy, 8, visited with Santa at a military base holiday party. He pointed back over his shoulder and whispered to Santa, "My sister's back there and is gonna' try to get me moved to the naughty list." He added, "You'll know her when she gets up here, she's such a drama queen." He continued, "Please don't buy into her act, please, oh and do you like scotch?"

A little boy, 6, asked Santa if, "I can run some bad stuff by you to see if it's bad enough for the naughty list or not."

A boy, 7, stopped to see Santa at his local Boys and Girls Club Christmas party. He had his cell phone out and said, "Can you send me a text if I made the nice list this month, so I can still be a little naughty, huh?"

A boy, 7, came to see Santa at a Boys & Girls Club Christmas party and inquired, "Is there like a Santa naughty and nice list app so I can see where I stand during the year?"

A boy, 7, blurted out to Santa, "Wow, I been thinking, how do you keep track of all the bad stuff we do." Santa told the boy it was Christmas magic. The boy replied, "Hmmmmm, shoulda' figured it'd be some special stuff I can't figure out!"

A boy, 5, visited with Santa at a National Guard children's holiday party. "I get blamed for everythings," he said, raising his arms over his head. "I might just get a private 'dective you know," he added.

A little boy, 7, came up to Santa and asked, "Can you define good for me?" He added, "I'm pretty much perfect, so I just wanted to make sure of your definition."

A little boy asked Santa, "They all call me troublesome. That means I'm only in some trouble, right?" How do I start to explain that one?

A boy, 5, said to Santa with a big, big smile on his face, "I can leave lots of extra cookies for you if it helps my cause!"

A boy, 7, came to see Santa at his school holiday pageant. "I been thinking, could you create a bad stuff app that has like a scale of 1 to 10 so you can double check how bad things are before you do 'em," he asked? He added, "I think it would be really, really helpful, just saying."

A little boy stopped to see Santa and had kind of a sheepish look on his face. He dragged his shoe back and forth on the stage, finally looked up and said, "Is there a way to get extra credit if you're in real trouble on the naughty list?"

A boy, 7, visited Santa at his local Boys and Girls Club. He said, "My grandpa said I might be able to come back strong in December if I stop pulling my sisters hair." I told him that there was still lots of time, almost 5 weeks, in which to have a good chance to get on the nice list. He got very excited and declared, "Wow, that would be a first!"

CHAPTER 18

Hospitals

Visiting children in hospitals is often one of the hardest parts of the role. It's also one of the most rewarding. In most cases, the kids are on the mend and Santa provides good cheer, hope for a quick recovery and lots of fun. In addition to visiting children one on one who are unable to leave their hospital rooms, lots of medical facilities will have a gathering of young patients and their families plus staff in a meeting room. These get togethers are wonderful right before the holidays. Christmas Eve and Christmas Day are especially good times to bring some joy to those confined to a hospital. More challenging is to visit children who have serious medical issues or are in various stages of their last days and weeks. This is where comfort, hope, human kindness, and empathy are greatly needed. I am always amazed at the genuine care given by medical staff and first responders. Santa's cap off to doctors, nurses, physicians assistants, social service workers, technicians, office staff, EMT's, police, fire, and other agencies. The caregivers and first responders are absolutely priceless!

Santa asked a little girl in a children's wing of a hospital what she wanted to be when she grew up. She pointed to her nurse. "Why do you want to be a nurse," I asked. She got all excited and replied, "I get to hand out the new babies." She continued, "When the mommies and daddies come in to pick up the baby they ordered, I give them one, 'course I'll keep cute ones for me!"

A boy, 7, was in the hospital with two broken legs from a bicycle accident with a car. "The car won, I guess," he said. When I asked what he would like for Christmas, he replied, "Can you sign both my casts?" I got out my trusty green and red sharpie markers and signed both. He beamed and said, "Cool, now I can sell 'em on eBay."

A girl, 4, looked at Santa with sad eyes and announced, "I's in 'pospital, I's sicky."

Santa was talking with a little boy when his nurse came in. The boy pointed to her and said, "I like her." The nurse smiled. Santa said that nurses help people to get well when they are in the hospital. The boy replied, "Yea, I know, but I think I gotta' problem." He looked at Santa and his nurse and asked, "Is my head crooked?" Both Santa and his nurse looked at each other and asked the boy why he asked. He replied, "Daddy says I better get my head on straight or no presents for Christmas!" Ah, that problem.

A girl, 6, visited with Santa at the children's wing of her local hospital. She told Santa she would like to be a nurse when she grew up. I asked her what she would do in her new job. She replied, "If people are nice, I'd read them books." Then she added, "If they were mean, I'd give them a sleeping pill."

Santa stopped to see a little boy who had a huge stain at the top of his hospital shirt. When I asked him what happened, he smiled and blurted out, "I was drinking juice and I forgot to swallow."

A little girl was in her hospital room when Santa came to see her. She said, "The doctor said I'm gonna' be all better 'cause I'm getting a new diet, looks like you need one too!"

A little boy visited with Santa at a local children's hospital. When Santa asked him if he needed anything, the boy replied, "Yes, my puppy Chester." I told him I was sure Chester missed him too. The boy said, "Oh yea, that too, but there's all kinds of stuff on the food tray I don't like and no place to hide it." Apparently, Chester takes care of that problem for him at home!

Santa asked a little girl what she would like for Christmas. She replied, "Brand new tonsils every year." She added, "That way I can keep coming here and eat popsicles."

A boy, 6, asked, "When you're sick, does Mrs. Claus give you shots in the butt too?"

A little girl said she needed to whisper something to Santa. I leaned down close, and she said, "They keep bringing me this green stuff to eat, but I don't think it's all dead yet, it wiggles." A first-time jello eater, I guess.

A little boy in a children's section of a rural hospital said, "Mommy told me to make sure I don't wet the bed here 'cause it's not my house."

A girl, 6, was in hospital and a day away from a serious surgery. She looked at Santa and asked, "Do you know Jesus?" I told her yes. She continued, "Can you pray to him for me to be all better?" I told her we could pray right there. Her nurse, parents, grandparents, and a lab technician were all in the room at the time. She looked at me and said, "I can't kneel down 'cause it hurts." I told her it was OK, Santa would do it for her and knelt at her bedside. We prayed together. When I got up, she beamed at her parents and said, "I bet it's gonna' be OK now." Smiles all around.

A little boy told Santa he wanted to be a doctor when he grew up, pointing to his physician. The doctor beamed as the boy continued, "You come in rooms with a piece of paper, hold your chin and go hmmmmmm."

A boy, 6, told Santa being in the hospital was not so bad. "They bring you juice boxes, ice cream and pretty nurses!"

A girl, 6, was in a critical care section of a local hospital. She looked up and said, "I'm gonna' be up in the sky like you are on Christmas Eve." Her parents had told me in advance that she was passing from an inoperable illness. I told her that it was really very beautiful in the sky with clouds, rainbows, sunrises, and sunsets. She smiled a weak smile and said, "I'll wave when you go by, OK?" I told her that would be wonderful, and I would always wave back. We talked some more, and she fell asleep, hopefully dreaming of beautiful clouds, rainbows, sunrises, and sunsets.

A girl, 6, told Santa that she wanted to be a nurse now that she was being cared for in the hospital. Santa asked her how she would care for him if he had a bad cold. "Oh, you're on your own, I don't want to catch it," she replied.

A boy, 6, told Santa he had a secret. "I think the doctor is like a superhero or somethin'," he said. I asked, "How do you know?" He replied, "Well, he has this thing round his neck, and he puts it on my chest and can see inside my chest with his ears." After all these years, I finally know how a stethoscope works!

A little girl whispered to Santa, "You can tell me, is it true doctor's keep all the bestest' babies for them?"

A boy, 7, was in the children's wing of an area hospital while Santa was visiting. A nurse came in and asked the boy which arm he would like his shot in. The boy pointed to Santa and replied, "His!"

A little boy told Santa, "This place is really cool, I get to wear PJ's all the time."

A girl, 6, told Santa she had decided she was going to be a nurse when she grew up. I asked her if she knew what all nurses did. "Oh, yes, they come in, bring you juice and jello and say, I'll be right back," was her reply.

A boy was in the hospital as Santa made his rounds. When Santa asked him what he would like to have for Christmas, the boy pointed to his doctor who was in the room seeing another patient. "Ask him 'cause he's gonna' take something out a me and I need you to bring me a new one to put back in," the boy replied.

A boy talked with Santa in the children's section of his local hospital. His sister was in the room, and they had been picking on each other for a while. She went out of the room to get something to eat. The boy said, "I been thinking that I'd like to be one of those jubilant delinquents for Christmas." Santa asked him to explain. The boy replied, "Well, I think they get to go away for a long time, so for me, the further away from my sister the better." Not quite sure that's how it all works.

A little girl visited with Santa and said all she wanted for Christmas was to be able to go home from the hospital and play with her new puppy. Santa assured her she was on the mend and would soon be able to be back home. She smiled and replied, "That's good 'cause he's not toilet trained and probably made quite a mess."

A little boy, 5, gave Santa the once over when he came into his hospital room and blurted out, "Geez, who dressed you this mornin'?"

Santa stopped to talk with a little boy sharing a room with an older boy at his local hospital. The boy told Santa he needed to whisper something to him. Santa leaned in close, and the little guy said, "Do you know if they let ducks bring in here?" Santa was a little confused and asked the boy to explain more. He whispered, "That boys daddy was just here and said he needed to get his ducks in a row for Christmas." Ah, mystery solved!

A little girl, 6, asked Santa if nurses or elves get paid more. Santa told her that nurses did because they had to go to school for a long time and had to take extra good care of all their patients like her. "But the elves have to make all the fun toys," she replied. She got me with that one.

CHAPTER 19

Parents and Grandparents

Children coming to visit Santa Claus often arrive with their parents, grandparents or other family members like aunts, uncles, and older siblings. Who accompanies kids often changes the dynamics of the visit. Kids often can be more open and forthcoming when they are with friends or alone, if old enough. I encourage family members to stand back a bit so the child can feel they are having some exclusive time with Santa. Parents are often looking for clues to what their children want for Christmas. Other than writing a letter to Santa, many times kids will only tell Santa their true wishes. In these cases, I can tell when parents are leaning in to hear things. My technique is to repeat the wish in a louder Santa voice so the family members can hear and take note. Often, I see parents look at each other with puzzled faces wondering where that wish came from. I've been thanked many, many times by family members that didn't have a clue where to begin shopping before our visit. I'm often asked if Santa "promises" to fulfill Christmas wishes. I use the phrase, "Santa will do his best for you," especially if it's a pricey or outlandish wish. What kids say to Santa is often totally unfiltered. It's my favorite part of the experience listening to what's blurted out or declared by these little characters. A word or phrase from kids such as, "So..." or "I been thinkin'" gives me notice to prepare myself to listen carefully and get a good answer ready. Children can also cause horrified and nervous looks from the family members due to their brutal honesty. "You told me to be honest" or "You said to always tell the truth," is often the comeback from a child when being admonished for what comes out. I've also received countless lists, drawings, cards, paintings and carefully printed letters with unfortunate misspellings, wild wishes, and embarrassing revelations. I wish I had saved them all to share. Here are a few stories I did write down over the years that I can share.

A little boy came to visit Santa at his local church Christmas pageant. He looked up and said with a very serious tone in his voice, "Do you know who I belong to?" I asked him to tell me more about his question. He pointed to his parents who were with him and replied, "Well, when I'm bad, they tell me I might not be theirs." Mom and dad both put their heads in their hands with that one.

A girl, 7, was with her grandparents at an area military base holiday party. She looked at Santa, back at her grandfather, back to Santa and blurted out, "Wow, nana's right, you guys really are older than dirt!" Grandma said, "I'll be right back, going to get some refreshments."

A little boy was with his parents as he came to talk to Santa. He told Santa that he "Gets no respect." I asked him to explain. He replied, "Well, I told mommy and daddy I want six brothers and six sisters and all they does' is laugh," he replied. "See," he said, pointing to his parents who were doubled over in laughter. "I might as well get married and have 'em myself," he said disgustedly.

A little girl, 5, told Santa that she had a "Duck named Robert." Santa asked if she liked her pet. She sadly replied, "Yes, but I think we're gonna' eat him for Christmas!"

A boy stopped to see Santa with his parents at a Boys and Girls Club holiday party. When I asked if he had any brothers or sisters, he replied, "No." He looked at his mom and dad, pointed to them and said, "I must be really special 'cause they said I'm enough for anybody."

A girl, 7, came to see Santa with her parents at the local fire department children's holiday party. She told me that she wanted to have a little brother and sister for Christmas. I asked her what her parents thought about it. She replied, "Well, daddy mixes a martini with triple olives and mommy pours a glass of wine." Her parents roared in laughter. I decided to leave it there.

A boy, 6, visited Santa and asked if he got to see the stork up in the sky flying by with new babies. Santa asked him what he was checking on. The boy looked at his grandpa and said, "Well, he said I mighta' been dropped on my head, so, I figured it was the storks' fault."

A little boy was with his parents and said to Santa, "I want a baby brother for Christmas to boss around." Before Santa could respond, the boy added, "Mommy said to ask my daddy, but what's he got to do with it?" This one was going to take a while!

A girl came into a Boys and Girls Club children's Christmas party at the very last minute and all out of breath. She stood in front of Santa with her hands on her hips and declared, "I didn't think we were going to make it in time." She pointed to her grandfather and added, "It took forever to get here 'cause grandpa always takes the long, short cuts."

A little boy climbed up the steps to the stage at a National Guard children's Christmas event to talk to Santa. He was with his grandparents. He looked at Santa and said, "My grandpa's very, very, very old like you." His grandparents were a bit embarrassed as the boy added, "I'm not sure his age, but we've had him a very long time."

A little girl visited Santa and said her wish was that her mommy would speed up saying grace before dinner because it always gets cold. "Plus, Grace never shows up anyways!"

A little boy came to see Santa and had a whole list of Christmas wishes. Santa asked if he had any brothers or sisters. The boy said he did not. I asked if he would like a brother. He looked over at his parents and replied, "Probably not, they're too old." His parents were stunned as he added, "Dads like 30 and mom's, I don't know, like 60 or 70." I am thinking there was no stop at the ice cream store on the way home that day!

A boy, 6, stopped to see Santa with his older sister who was pregnant. I asked him if he knew if his sister's baby was going to be a little boy or girl. He looked up and replied, "Yea, not yet, so I don't know if I'm gonna' be a aunt or a uncle."

A little boy had at the top of his Christmas wish list lots of hair and Elmer's glue. Santa inquired about the unique wish. The boy pointed to his balding grandfather and said, "It's for papa!"

A girl came to see Santa at a fire department children's holiday party. She asked Santa if she could whisper in his ear since she was with her mom. Santa said yes, and the little girl leaned near his ear. "I think my daddy's a fortune teller guy," she said. I asked her for more information. "Well, he said if my four brothers don't behave, mommy's gonna' be in a nervous wreck," she added.

A little boy was with his parents at a Boys and Girls Club holiday party. He was all dressed up in a white shirt, black pants, red bow tie, red and green vest, and shiny new black shoes. He blurted out, "This better be worth it 'cause I even had to take a extra bath."

A little girl stopped to visit with Santa at her local church Christmas pageant party. She looked up and said, "Can you tell me how many cookies you expect to eat Christmas Eve?" I asked her to explain more. "I wanna' know so I can save the rest for grandpa and me," she said pointing to her proud grandfather. "That's my girl," he said.

A boy, 7, told Santa that his only Christmas wish was to be able to stay up later at night. I asked him to tell me more. He replied, "Well, all the really cool TV shows are on then, you know, with fights and sexy stuff." Mom, standing nearby, surely took note.

A boy came to visit with Santa with his mom and dad. They were all excited for their son's first face to face with jolly old Saint Nick. They had their cellphones out to take photos and a video and patiently waited to hear his wish list. When Santa asked what his parents did, the boy replied, "Mommy drinks wine, daddy drinks beer, then they go in the bedroom, shut the door and make all kinds of noises." Not quite sure if that was what any of us were expecting!

A little boy, 4, came to see Santa for the very first time with his grandparents. When Santa asked what he would like for Christmas, the boy looked up and said, "Not sure I'm 'spossed to say." I asked him to explain if he could. He looked up again with a confused look on his face and replied, "I'm not 'spossed to spill the beans 'bout us."

A little girl stopped to see Santa at her local school Christmas play after party. I asked her what she wanted to be when she grew up. She said she wanted to be a homemaker just like her mommy, pointing to her mom. Mom smiled as the girl continued, "You just drink wine with your girlfriends all day long, then order pizza for dinner." Again, not sure either of us saw that coming.

A little boy visited Santa at his local sheriff's office children's Christmas party. He was with his grandparents. When I asked him what he would like to be when he grew up, he thought for a bit and finally said, "A bull." I was surprised by that and asked him to explain. He said, "Well, grandpa always says I'm full of it, so I may's well be that."

A boy, 5, was with his grandparents as he came to see Santa for the first time. He was quite talkative. My favorite revelation of his was that his mommy and daddy got him at a store. "I think I was on sale," he said. Grandpa roared at that one, grandma not so much.

A little boy was with his dad at a military base children's Christmas party. He had a very serious look on his face. I could tell dad was a bit stressed about what his young son might come out with. Finally, the boy asked, "Do you know where I came from?" Before I could answer that question of all questions, he saved the day as he added, "My new buddy Jacob says he's from Oregon, so I just need to know."

Twin brothers, 5, came to see Santa with their parents. They were both decked out in matching reindeer sweaters, freshly cut hair and new sneakers. "So, when you see the stork up there flying around, tell him we want more brothers, OK," said the first. Mom and dad looked at each other nervously. "Yea, like a dozen or so, then we can have our own football team!" said the second.

A little girl told Santa that she would like to have a baby sister so they could play with dolls together. Mom and dad were with her at the children's Christmas party. She looked at them and added, "I think I heard we get one after they take a nap together."

A little boy was with his older brother at a holiday party. He looked at Santa and blurted out, "Eric brought me 'cause my parents wanted to get rid a' me for the day."

A boy, 6, came to his local school Christmas pageant with his mom. He told Santa he had a secret. He leaned in close to Santa's ear and said, "I think mommy cheats on how many candles she puts on her birthday cake."

A little girl was with her parents at a church Christmas event. She pointed to her parents and said, "That's my mommy and my daddy. They got together and here I am, the end."

A girl, 6, stopped to see Santa with her parents. She said, "I got a question for you." I asked what it was. She pointed to her mom and said, "Mom's on a diet, you think it's working?" I hesitated and she added, "I asked daddy and he said mummy's the word." I decided to pass as well!

A boy, 6, visited Santa at a local Boys and Girls Club with his grandparents. I asked him if he would ever like to have any brothers or sisters. He replied, "Nope, they'd just cut into my allowance." Grandpa roared at that one.

A little boy came to see Santa and said he had new pants on. I told him they looked really nice. The boy leaned in and whispered, "Mommy told me not to scratch, even if it itches." Secret's safe with me!

A little girl, 3, stopped to see Santa with her parents at her local church Christmas pageant. She had a brand-new dress on, new shoes and a cute bow in her hair. She rocked back and forth for a while. She finally looked up and said, "Are you Jesus?"

A little boy visited Santa at his local police department's children's holiday party. His grandparents were with him. He leaned in close to Santa's ear and said, "I like playing cards with my grandma 'cause I think she lets me win." Good to know.

A girl, 5, told Santa that her mommy was a schoolteacher. Her mom stood by beaming. Santa asked what her mommy liked about teaching. The girl replied, "Everything 'cept the kids."

A boy, 6, came to visit with Santa at his local Boys and Girls Club. He was with his dad. When I asked him what his daddy was like? The little guy boasted, "Oh, he's just like me, he's irresistible to the ladies!" His dad cracked up at that one.

CHAPTER 20

But, Why?

Sometimes it starts at age 3, but 4 and 5 for sure. It's every parent's special age when every answer you give to your child is followed by, "but, why?" You can only follow up with "because" or "because I said so" for so long. And who can forget the first time a child asks, "So, where do babies come from?" And the parents' response is typically, "Ask your father" or "Ask your mother." It's wonderful that children are inquisitive and in wonder with everything going on around them. Inquiring minds want to know more, even at a young age. Santa gets his fair share of the "but, whys" too. Probably an inordinate amount, actually. Flying reindeer, living at the North Pole, a red sleigh, fluffy red suit and hat, long white beard and tons of elves give children lots of things to question, "but, why!"

A little boy came to see Santa at his local church children's Christmas pageant. He was dressed as one of the Wise Men and was starring at his hands. I was not sure where this was headed. Finally, he spoke, "Why do they keep saying my hands are full, I don't see nothin'." I asked him to tell me more. "Well, mommy and daddy are always saying I'm a hands full," he replied. I should have seen that one coming.

A girl, 6, visited Santa and said, "Why do my mommy and daddy keep saying I'm not very responsible; I'm just an amateur kid, right?"

A boy, 6, stopped to see Santa and asked, "So why do they call it menopause if it's for ladies." Before I could respond, he added, "Seems to me that girls get everything cool."

A boy came to see Santa and said, "Why is it mommy thinks my daddy is an expert?" I asked him to tell me more. "Well, when I ask her stuff like where babies come from and all that, she says to go ask your father," he explained.

A little girl was missing two of her front teeth when she came to visit Santa. "Why do my teeth keep falling out, am I defective," she asked. I assured her that new, bigger teeth were coming right behind the ones that came out. "So, when the bigger ones fall out too, do I get more money from the tooth fairy cause they're bigger ones," she asked. I was going to tell her to ask her dentist!

A little boy, 6, asked Santa, "Why do I have to go to sleep Christmas Eve and wait so long to get to open my presents?" I told him Santa needed time to get to all the boys and girls houses that night. "But, why" he asked again. I smiled and told him he needed his sleep to grow up big and strong. He replied, "I'm OK being a little smaller and weaker to get my toys faster." Ah, yes, young minds at work!

A girl stopped to see Santa at her local Boys and Girls Club Christmas party. She looked up at Santa and said, "Why does my teacher say to stop talking till it's my turn?" Before I could respond, she added, "So, when's it my turn?"

A boy visited with Santa and told him he had four older brothers. Santa asked him what his favorite game was. The boy thought for a bit and finally said, "It used to be hide and seek." I asked him what changed things. The boy replied, "Why am I always 'it'?"

A little boy came to see Santa at his local fire department children's holiday party. He stood in front of Santa and asked, "Why do I have to wait till Christmas morning if you're here and I'm here already?" Hard to argue with that logic.

A little girl visited with Santa and asked, "Why do I have to eat on a grown-up plate when I'm little?" She added, "I think I should have a little plate so less room for veggies."

A boy, 6, told Santa he had a lot of questions. I got myself prepared and sat back for the first round. "Why do I have to brush my teeth when I just gotta' do it all over again," he asked. Santa told him it was to keep his teeth and gums healthy. He replied, "Why, they fall out anyway." Santa told him it was natural for smaller children's teeth to be replaced by bigger teeth. "But, why do I have to take a bath if I just have to take another one that week?" His mom said, "Honey, there's a lot of children here today that Santa needs to see, so why don't you just give him your Christmas wish list." The little boy looked at her and replied, "What's the use, I didn't get that pony last year!"

"I gotta' question," said a little girl at her local church Christmas pageant. Santa told her to go ahead and ask it. "OK, so, I got a younger sister and a' older sister, "she said. "So, does that mean I'm middle-aged cause mommy says she's middle-aged and she's really old!"

A little boy marched up the steps to the stage at a military base children's Christmas party. He stood right in front of Santa, raised his arms over his head and asked, "Why do I always barf when I eat too much cake and ice cream, but not when I eat too much veggies?

A girl told Santa all about her Christmas wishes and plans for the holidays. She said she would be visiting her grandparents and singing in the church children's choir. Then she said, "I got one question for you Mr. Santa." She added, "When do I get my stuff?"

A boy, 6, came up to Santa all in a panic and said, "I really need your help." Santa asked him what he could do for him. The boy said he had a new shirt on, his very first dress shirt. He said his mom told him not to be messy and leave his shirt tail out. "Santa, I can't find any tail?"

A little girl was at a breakfast with Santa children's event. When it was her turn, Santa asked her what her wish was. She looked at him sleepy-eyed and replied, "To go back to bed."

A boy, 6, visited with Santa with a frantic look on his face. I figured it had to do with the naughty list, but alas, I was wrong. "Santa, why do they bury people when they stop breathing?" Before I could reply, he added, "'Cause I like to practice holding my breath and I don't want nobody to make a mistake!"

A little boy told Santa that he had just started school that fall. Santa asked him how he liked it so far. The boy looked up and said, "Not so much." I asked him what he would do to change school if he could. He replied, "No teachers!"

A little girl came to see Santa and when asked what her Christmas wish was replied, "I wanna' be five, I'm really done with being four, you know."

A boy, 6, stopped to talk with Santa and said he had a major problem with his older sister. I asked him what the issue was. He replied, "Well, she keeps tellin' me to zip it and I look and my zippers still up on my pants."

A little boy visited with Santa at a military base children's Christmas party. He said he had a problem with his four older brothers when they played army games. I asked him what the problem was. He sadly replied, "Why am I always the 'emeny'?"

A girl, 6, told Santa her only wish was for her teeth to keep falling out all her life so she could only eat "popsicles, jello and ice cream."

A little boy, at a fire department children's Christmas party, told Santa that he had a secret. "When I came here today, I had my pants on backwards," he whispered. He added, "I found out when I had to pee."

CHAPTER 21

Kids' Jokes

Kids love to tell Santa Claus their favorite jokes. Often, they can't wait to be introduced to Santa by the elves and just start right in. Some of the jokes are pretty corny to adults but not to the young storytellers. Many times, they leave parts out or start laughing before the joke is finished. Often, they totally forget the punchline. I'm not sure why they feel so comfortable telling their jokes to Santa, but I often hear 3 or 4 at every appearance. Maybe it's the fact that Santa Claus is viewed as a non-judgmental and safe adult to share these jokes with. Many, many times the jokes are the same or very similar. The kids really look for Santa's reaction, so this is one opportunity for me to let out a good, hearty laugh. I'm also not sure exactly where the jokes come from. TV, school friends, siblings and books are probably the main sources. It's one of my favorite things to observe and be part of. I guess this is where little comedians are born or at least try out their new material.

A boy, 7, came up to Santa at a National Guard children's Christmas party, his arms folded in front of his chest. He said, "Guess why you should never mess with Santa, Santa?" Without waiting for me to reply, he said, "'Cause you got a black belt!"

A brother and sister, 7 and 8, ran up the steps at a Boys and Girls Club holiday party and blurted out in unison, "Santa, Santa, guess what's you and Mrs. Claus' nationality?" I knew it was coming, but I let them have their fun. "Why, I don't know what it would be," I replied. They beamed and said, "You're both North Polish, get it!!!" We'll have to double check that with the Ancestry website.

A little girl, 6, was giggling at a community center party when she asked me, "Knock, knock?" I replied, "Who's there?" She said, "Carrie." I replied, "Carrie, who?" She replied, "Will you carry my schoolbooks for me, he, he."

Two twin brothers, 6, were playfully punching each other waiting in line at a military base recreation hall. When they got up to Santa, they asked, "Santa, what do you get when you cross a fish with an elephant?" It's swimming trunks, silly!"

A boy, 7, proudly asked, "Santa, Santa, what did one pencil say to the other pencil?" He said, "You're really looking sharp." He could not contain himself, so he asked further, "Guess where pencils go when they go on vacation?" "Pennsylvania, that's where."

A boy, 7, came up to Santa at a school holiday party. He asked, "What do people in prison use to call each other?" "It's cellphones, ha, ha, cellphones, get it?"

A girl, 6, told Santa the best way to talk to fishes is to drop them a line.

A boy, 8, at a church Christmas party asked Santa what one pig said to the other pig while playing basketball. "Stop hogging the ball!" he said.

Two brothers, 6 and 7, ran up the steps of the Santa stage at a Fire department auxiliary children's party and did their own knock knock joke. "Knock, knock," one said. "Who's there," said the other. "Les," he replied. "Les, who?" "Les one there is a rotten egg!"

A girl, 7, asked Santa why the credit card went to prison. "'Cause it was guilty as charged," she added, busting up laughing.

A boy, 6, came to see Santa at the local Boys and Girls Club party. He asked, "Where do boats go when they get all sick?" He said, "They go to the dock!"

A little girl asked Santa what her cats' favorite song is? "It's three blind mice, Santa!"

A boy, 6, came to see Santa with his best buddy both decked out in their favorite NFL sweatshirts. The one boy said, "Santa, why do you think the football coach went to the bank?" His friend answered, "He needed to get his quarter back!"

A girl, 7, stopped to see Santa at the Police department children's Christmas party. She was already laughing when she said, "I know what all your elves eat for breakfast at the North Pole, Santa." "Frosted Flakes, that's what," she added.

A little boy, 6, asked Santa why it's so easy for elephants to get jobs. "'Cause they'll just work for peanuts, that's why!"

A girl, 7, asked Santa if he heard about a frog's car that broke down on the highway. "It had to be toad away," she said.

Two brothers, 6 and 8, asked Santa what the jack said to the car? "Can I give you a lift?"

A little girl, 6, came to see Santa at her school holiday party. She was grinning from ear to ear as she asked Santa what the smartest kind of bee is. "A spelling bee, isn't that funny."

A boy, 6, asked Santa why all the pillows went to see the doctor. "It's 'cause they were all stuffed up!"

A boy, 7, was at a military base children's Christmas party. He came up to the stage and told Santa, "Guess what the pirate's kids' favorite subject in school is?" "It's Arrrrrrt."

A boy, 8, asked Santa, "Why do you think my little brother ate his homework?" "It's 'cause my mom told him it was a piece of cake!"

A little girl was giggling all the way up the steps to see Santa. "Santa, Santa, what's the bestest time to go see the dentist?" She said, "It's tooth-hurty, that's when, ha, ha."

A boy, 7, came to see Santa at a church children's holiday party. He asked, "Hey Santa, what did the lawyer name his new baby daughter?" The boy added, "He named her, Sue, get it, Sue!"

Two twin sisters, 7, could not wait to get to the head of the line to see Santa. When it was finally their turn, they both said in unison, "Santa, guess why the lettuce was always winning all of the races?" "Because it was always a head, silly!"

A boy, 7, was with his buddy at a church holiday party. The boy was grinning from ear to ear. "Santa, guess what the chocolate chip cookie said when he went to the doctor? "He said he was feeling a little bit crummy."

A little girl, 7, was all excited for her chance to see Santa Claus at her church children's Christmas pageant event. She proudly came up and said, "Do you know why the King went to see the dentist?" She answered, "'Cause he wanted to get all of his teeth crowned, that's why."

"Santa, Santa, what did the lemon say to the nurse when he went to the doctor's office? The boy, 6, could hardly wait to tell Santa the punch line. Then, he forgot it and his mom had to lean over and remind him. "Oh, yea, I need some Lemon-Aid!"

Two sisters, 6 and 7, asked Santa what the stick of butter said to the jar of peanut butter. They started giggling and holding their stomachs. I was not sure if they would even be able to finish the joke. Finally, they stopped laughing long enough to say, "I think you're NUTS!"

Two twin brothers, 6, came running down the hall at a military base recreation center and had their knock-knock joke ready. The first boy said, "Knock-knock?" The second boy replied, "Who's there?" "Ken." "Ken, who?" "Ken you come out and play with me," said the brother. They were not done yet. The first boy started back in, "Knock-knock." "Who's there?" asked his brother. "Peas." "Peas who?" "Peas, can you come out and play with me," his brother finished. I was not sure how long this was going to go on. Fortunately, their grandmother came up and winked at me. She announced, "Let's go you two, Santa's got lots of other children to get to." Plus, lots more jokes to hear!

Three brothers visited Santa with their mom. The oldest said to Santa, "What do you think our mom's favorite Christmas song is?" He looked over at his mom, turned back to Santa and said, "It's Silent Night for sure."

A little girl, 5, was all decked out in her red and green party dress at a children's party at a nursing home where her grandparents were. She said to Santa, "Do you know who brings little kittens to kids at Christmas?" I smiled and let her finish, "It's Santa Claws, silly."

A boy, 6, asked Santa where the Easter bunny goes when he goes out to eat. "IHOP, that's where," he added.

Two brothers, 6 and 8, asked Santa what sheep do when they go to Karate class. "They do lamb chops, get it!"

A girl, 7, was very excited to come and visit with Santa at her local children's hospital's holiday celebration. She said, "Santa, do you know what spiders do on their computers?" She added, "They make websites."

A little girl, 5, came with her grandmother to see Santa at a church holiday event. They were so cute, walking and holding hands. "Tell Santa your joke, honey," said her grandmother. The girl was a little shy, so I bent down a bit to be closer for her. She looked up and said, "What's a fairy's name who won't take her bath?" I told her I didn't know what it would be. "Her name is Stinker Bell," the girl replied. I think they had rehearsed that one.

A boy, 7, asked Santa why you just cannot believe what a balloon says. He added, "'Cause they're so full of hot air, that's why!"

A boy, 6, could not wait to share his favorite joke with Santa. "Guess why the doggie was all sad, Santa?" He added, "It's 'cause his life was so ruff."

A girl, 5, asked Santa what kind of car Minnie Mouse drives. "It's a Minnie Van," she said. Should have seen that one coming, get it, a van coming! OK, I'll just stick to being Santa, I promise.

A little girl came to see Santa at a community center Christmas party. "Santa, what did the candy use when it broke its leg?" she asked. "A candy cane," she added.

A boy, 6, asked Santa what the fastest peanut butter in the world is. "It's Jiffy!"

Two girls, best friends, visited Santa at a military base Christmas party. The first girl said, "Do you know what the blanket said to the bed, Santa?" I knew I was double-teamed so I let them go for it. "Don't worry, I got you covered, tee-hee," she said.

Two brothers, 6 and 7, raced up the steps to the stage to see Santa at an outdoor Christmas party in Ewa Beach, Hawaii on Oahu Island. "Santa, Santa, we got jokes for you," said one boy. "Do you know what happened when two huge waves raced each other in the ocean?" The second boy replied, "They tide, get it, tide!!!" "I got another one," said the first brother. "What do you call a polar bear here in Ewa?" He answered, "You call him LOST!" They both busted up laughing and snorting. The second boy jumped back in, "Santa, what kinda tree here can fit in your hand?" "A palm tree, that's what, a palm tree," he said. "Oh, Oh, Santa, what did the palm tree wear to the beach," the first boy asked? "His swimming trunks," he said. Look out famed island comedians Frank De Lima and Andy Bumatai, there is a new bunch of comics coming from Ewa Beach!!!

A girl, 7, asked Santa what the mommy horse said to the little boy pony? "She told him to stop horsing around." She added, "Oh, and what did the pony say when it was sick?" "Sorry, but I'm a little hoarse today," she said.

Two boys, good buddies, were all excited to come and see Santa at their local Fire department party. "Hey Santa, guess what one toilet said to the other toilet?" "You look all flushed," his friend added. "Oh, yea, I got another one," said the first boy. "Why was the boy running around his bed in his bedroom?" He finished, "'Cause he was catching up on his sleep."

A little girl, 6, visited Santa at a Veteran's hospital holiday party. She smiled and said, "Santa, Santa, do you know how to tell if the moon is done eating dinner?" "Cause it's full," she said.

A boy, 7, said to Santa, "Santa, do you know why I threw my alarm clock out the window on Christmas eve?" I knew what was coming but let him finish the punchline anyway. "It's 'cause I wanted to see time fly," he said. "That way it would be Christmas day, faster too," he added.

"Santa, Santa, I got a joke for you," said the little boy. "What's the man in the moons favorite candy?" He added, "A Mars Bar, that's what."

A little girl, 5, came to see Santa at a Boys and Girls Club Christmas party. She could hardly contain herself. She was with her older brother. He said, "She's got this joke and has been rehearsing and rehearsing it to tell you." She started in, "What did baby corn say to mommy corn?" She started giggling and I was not sure she would be able to finish it. Finally, she stopped laughing and said, "Where's popcorn?" She started laughing again, then pointed to her big brother. He finished the joke off his big part adding, "Isn't that CORNY Santa!!!"

Well, as they say, I guess the joke's truly on me!

CHAPTER 22

The Doubters

In every child's young life, there comes a time, actually many, when doubt creeps in about whether or not there really is a Santa Claus. The number one question that arises is: how do you get to all of the houses on Christmas Eve? The standard Santa Claus answer of, "It's Christmas magic," only lasts so long before inquiring minds want more details. The parental response of; "If you don't believe, then maybe Santa won't come and you won't get any presents," doesn't settle the issue as well. Doubting starts in many ways: an older sibling, older friends, finding their parents' gift stash in the special hiding place before Christmas and many more. Lots of families have their own traditions that children are part of. One of the most popular, which helps eliminate the hiding place issue, is the parents buying two-thirds of the presents and having them wrapped under the tree during the last week or two. Then Santa brings the final gifts on Christmas Eve. That also helps with parents knowing what to buy up front. One of the funniest things for me to participate in is when children won't tell their Christmas wishes to their parents, only to Santa. The parents can be in the dark, often days before Christmas. I have learned to repeat their children's wishes loud enough for their parents to hear or share the wish list with one parent after the children leave. Parents often had no idea what their little ones really wanted. Writing a Christmas letter is a great way for parents to get a jump start on kids' wishes. In many families the age differences present a challenge in keeping the magic alive. Older siblings may let things slip that can ruin long held beliefs of younger children. I do enjoy watching older siblings coming to see Santa with their younger brothers and sisters and playing along. This happens a lot with service families as one parent may be deployed and the other working when the party is held. None the less, the doubters will always be there, we just all have to be creative with our responses and preparations for the special day.

A boy, 8, came to see Santa at a Boys and Girls Club Christmas party with a very worried look on his face. He finally got to the front of the line. "My best buddy says you ain't' real," he said. Santa smiled and replied, "What do you think young man?" He answered, "Whoa, that's a lot of pressure you know, I'm just a kid." Before I could go further, he added, "You know, let's just go with you're the real deal 'cause I don't want to be taking a lot of chances this early in my young life." Good idea, son, good thinking!

A girl, 9, visited with Santa at her local Boys and Girls Club Christmas party. She stood in front of him, gazed for a long time and finally said, "You got to be real, 'cause who would dress up like that if they didn't have to, just saying." Hmmmm, actually I thought I looked pretty spiffy that day.

A boy, 7, stopped to see Santa at a military base recreation center holiday party for children. He told Santa that some of his older brother's buddies said Santa was not true. Santa smiled and replied, "It doesn't matter what they believe, son, it's what you believe." The boy thought about that for a while and finally replied, "I'm thinking no Santa equals no presents. So, got it, I'm good to go, here's my list," he added. Problem solved!

A girl, 8, told Santa that she was trying to figure out how Christmas Eve worked with all the houses to visit and presents to deliver. Santa told her it was "Christmas magic." She smiled and replied, "So, like David Copperfield, right?" Santa told her, "Exactly, actually I taught him all his tricks." The girl's jaw dropped almost to the floor, and she said, "Wow, you are the REAL Santa!"

Twin brother and sister, 9, visited with Santa. They stood silent, but finally said, "Our neighbor said you weren't real." Santa asked if it was the neighbor on the right side or left side of their house. The boy looked at his sister and said, "Guess they get passed over this year, huh."

A boy, 8, told Santa that he had found his mom's Christmas gift hiding spot at his house. "So, now I'm like really confused," he said. Santa told the boy that he had so many children to visit and toys to put in the sleigh, that he needs help sometimes from moms and dads. The boy looked surprised and replied, "Geez, why didn't I think of that." He added, "Guess that's why you're Santa!"

A little girl, 3, came to see Santa with her older brother and asked to sit on his lap. She looked straight into my eyes and said, "I believes in you Mr. Santa man."

Two brothers, 8 and 9, stopped to see Santa at their local fire department children's holiday party. They stood right in front of Santa for a long time and looked back and forth at each other. They finally said in unison, "We ain't' riskin' it" and gave me their letters. More satisfied customers!

A boy, 8, came to visit Santa with a sheepish look on his face. He looked down at the ground for a while and swayed back and forth. He finally said, "I said some stuff 'bout you being real and all. I wanna' walk it all back," he added.

A girl, 7, visited Santa at her local church Christmas pageant party. She stood right in front of Santa and put her hands on her hips. She declared, "I figure I got lots to lose, right, so you're the real deal!"

A boy, 9, waited in line for a long time, got his chance to talk to Santa, but went to the back of the line again. He did this about three times. Finally, he marched up the steps to the stage, walked over to Santa and held his chin in his hand. "I'm sticking with real, my girlfriend just dumped me, and I can't afford to lose out on Christmas too," he said.

Twin brothers, 8, stopped to see Santa at their local sheriff's department children's Christmas party. They came up and looked me over a few times top to bottom, side to side. They looked at each other and back at me several more times. Almost in unison, they blurted out, "Works for me!" Both then handed me long lists of Christmas wishes.

A boy, 8, came to see Santa and asked how his sleigh and reindeer flew up in the sky on Christmas Eve. Santa replied that it was all "Christmas magic." The boy replied, "So, like superpowers and stuff like on Star Wars." Santa said yes, it was like that. The boy added, "Wow, could you bring me a droid then that could do my homework, please!"

A girl, 9, visited with Santa at her area Boys and Girls Club. She said she was starting to have some doubts about Santa being for real. She tried a question on me and asked, "What's my name?" I replied, "Ashley." She was shocked, told me all of her Christmas wishes and walked away shaking her head. I didn't have the heart to tell her that she had an adhesive nametag on!

Two boys, 8 and 9, talked to Santa at a church Christmas pageant. The older boy said, "So, here's the deal, our older brother says there is no Santa Claus." The younger boy added, "Yea, so then, do we get all of his Christmas presents 'cause we're totally with you!"

A girl, 9, told Santa that her older sister did not believe in Santa Claus anymore. "She thinks she's too cool for that," she said. I asked her what she thought. She was quiet for a bit and then replied, "What have I got to lose…except all my presents!" She then reached in her purse and pulled out her Christmas letter to Santa.

A boy, 8, at a military base recreation center stopped to see Santa. He blurted out, "Do you have like a certificate of authenticity?" My elf, an officer who knew him, was a bit shocked at the question. He looked at him and said, "Where did you learn those words, son?" The boy replied, "I looked it up on the internet, Sir." Santa smiled and said, "I'm part of Christmas magic young man, and I was authentic long before there even was an internet." The boy was stunned. He looked at Santa nervously and said, "roger that."

CHAPTER 23

It Could Only Happen to Santa!

I do not think anyone just wakes up one day and declares, "I'm going to be Santa Claus!" If anyone had told me, 25 years ago, (actually going on 29 in 2022) that I would spend 6 weeks every November & December as a volunteer Santa Claus, I would have just laughed and said, "Oh sure and then the Easter Bunny." Actually, it has been suggested numerous times that I would be a good Easter Bunny, but I digress.

All my life, I have been the embodiment of the phrase, "If it can happen, it will and happen to me." Same with the Luck of the Irish phrase: "If it can go wrong, it will and at the worst possible moment." So, when I thought about all of the possible things that could go wrong: costumes, changing in and out, driving to and from, on site mishaps, "accidents" by little ones, being ill, schedule changes, work obligations, overbooking … need I go on? It was quite the daunting list at best. Plus, I have been a tad "accident-prone" all my life which added to complicating the equation. But I have never allowed myself to get in the way of myself, so Santa Don was born, or created, or whatever.

A few of these stories are the only repeats from previous volumes because they are too much fun to require you to have to read the first two books. The repeats are rewritten as I remembered more and more details. I have added some new ones as well that I found when going through my 2, 000 cryptic notes. The second and last stories have become just about the most favorites of readers from previous years, so I had to include them.

A Home Visit Takes FOREVER!!!

I have only done Santa visits for four close friends over the twenty-eight, going on twenty-nine years that I have portrayed jolly old St. Nick. One of my absolute favorites was in Hawaii for a grandfather or "Papa," grandmother or "Tutu," their son, the father, mother and three children, ages five and a half, three and a half and one and a half. The grandfather had played the role of Santa for the children in the past. Each annual event consisted of everyone singing Christmas songs, then the grandfather would slip away and change. The final song, "Jingle Bells," was time for the grand entrance. Santa would then arrive with several sacks of presents for the Keiki (kids) to open. This year I would take over his role. "Papa" had set the whole thing up far in advance with me to fit into my schedule. He was so excited about the whole thing, especially since it would a total surprise to the kids. The plan was for me to arrive early, go into a master bedroom that was under renovation, and suit up as the young family arrived. Dinner for everyone would follow and I would join the family for that in effect as a new arrival after changing back into my street clothes.

The day finally came, I arrived, and went into the bedroom to change. Normally suiting up takes about a half hour or so. This day, however, would be quite different. Since the room was under renovation, there were few curtains on the large windows which faced out to the backyard. As I started to change, the father and his oldest son went outside in the backyard to toss a football around. Problem was that the son was on the end of the back-yard directly across from where I was changing. If he got close enough to the windows, he would see me, plus the two sacks filled with presents. Three times he missed the catch and the football bounced near the bedroom windows. Each time I dove to the floor in the space in between the two beds in order not to be seen. It was taking forever for me to suit up. Finally, the dad and son went inside to get ready to sing the traditional Christmas songs.

"Papa" stopped back to let me know they were ready and found me only half dressed. I told him what had happened, we laughed, and he went back into the family room to stall things a bit to let me finish. Finally ready, I took the two gift sacks, snuck out the bedroom sliding door and went around the side of the house to the front near an open window. The family all started singing "Jingle Bells," the traditional song for Santa to arrive. The kids knew it was time for "Papa" to slip away, but he stayed in the family room with them. Outside the window I said my Ho-Ho-Ho's in a booming voice and added, "This must be the right house." Everyone was surprised and looked at each other. The family adults told the two oldest kids to let Santa in the front door. They opened the door and there I was with two large sacks of gifts. The oldest boy stopped in his tracks, looked back at his grandfather, back at me, back at "Papa" and got a dazed, befuddled look on his face. He backed up and up and finally fell back into a chair, still unsure of what was happening. The daughter was the opposite. She invited me in and was giddy with joy. The youngest boy was sticking close to mom. I had thought that the oldest son would want to be my elf, but he was still spellbound and stayed in his chair at times looking back at "Papa" with a quizzical look on his face. I announced that Santa had been visiting the families' Uncle Barney in Los Angeles and he said there were three Keiki in Honolulu who were extra special good and deserved lots of extra presents. That was the purpose for my special early trip two weeks prior to Christmas day. The daughter jumped at the chance to be my elf and helped me hand out all the presents. She enjoyed stroking my beard plus lifting it up to look under it as lots of kids do.

After all the presents were handed out, the oldest son looked at his Uncle Preston who was empty handed and said, "Where's your present Uncle Pres?" Santa said, "No presents for him, he's been naughty." Preston announced, "I've been good Santa, plus I'm a 49er fan!" Santa turned thumbs down and said, "You need to be a Rainbow Warriors (University of Hawaii) fan instead!" Everyone cheered. To this day, the two oldest children will ask their uncle, "Still no presents for you Uncle Pres?" It has become a favorite line for the whole family. It was time for Santa to leave, I made my way out the front door and around to the back of the house to the bedroom to change. The kids ran to the front window of the house to see if they could catch a glimpse of the sleigh and reindeer. Just then a military helicopter flew by in the night sky and "Papa" told the kids Santa was on his way back to the North Pole! Mission accomplished.

A Run-in with the LAW!

Santa rarely double books himself and never, ever wears his suit in the car. Imagine me pulling up next to your car, especially with your children in it. How would you explain that one! Another volunteer Santa, who was a good friend, had suffered a slight stroke and I agreed to fill in for him at a children's event the same night as my already scheduled event. The problem was the parties could not have been further apart in Southern Nevada. His event was in Henderson, Nevada and mine in North Las Vegas, Nevada. I only had a half hour to drive from point A to point B. Fortunately Interstate 15 was a direct route between the two events, so staying in costume should be OK. Plus, it would be dark out when the first event ended, so I went for it! Since I have always been known for driving a bit over the speed limit, I also figured I would not be seen on the freeway as anything other than a red and white flash to any cars I passed. So, I left the first event, stayed in the Santa suit, and started to drive to the next event. Being in a real hurry, I made what is known as a California rolling stop (do not ask me why, it just is) at a stop sign before getting on the freeway. Of course, I got pulled over by a squad car. I was so very close to the freeway on ramp. With lights flashing and a strong white light illuminating my car, I rolled down the window and waited for my destiny. The officer approached and came to the driver's side window. He looked in and exclaimed, "Oh, Jesus." I replied, "No, just Santa Claus!" He did not look happy. Actually, he had this perplexed yet amused look on his face. After giving him my license, insurance, and registration, he went back to his car and checked it all out. He came back, handed me my documents, and slowly shook his head from side to side. Finally, he spoke and said, "How am I going to explain to my four kids at breakfast tomorrow morning that I ticketed Santa Claus?" I felt it was best to keep quiet at that point. "Can you see with all that on," he questioned. I assured him I could. I was only glad he did not ask me to explain why I was dressed that way, where I had been, where I was going, etc. So, he let me go with a warning. Actually, he also said, "Please, just go." I started to pull back into traffic and his lights went on again with a siren sound. I pulled over and he came back to the driver's window. I was afraid that he had reconsidered his merciful decision. He said "Can you come with me to the front of the squad car because I had to call in the stop and I need to close it out. This way the dash cam will record it, plus no one back at the station is going to believe this anyway!" We did, then he asked if he could take a few selfies for his kids. I said "You know, the reason I did the rolling stop was because I am really in a hurry. I may need an escort with flashing lights and siren if this takes any longer." He looked at me, all 6'2" of him and replied, "Don't push it, Santa." Point made and on my merry way I went.

A Tale of Make-up gone WRONG!

The entire Santa "suit-up," as we in the business call it, can take 30 to 40 minutes. I cannot grow a good enough natural beard and with all of the pulling on it, it is important you get it right. I was always looking for little ways to have a good costume. I recall a little girl, whom I had been Santa for at the same employee children's party for the past few years, noticing my watch and ring. She smiled and said, "I'm glad you're the same Santa, there's fake ones out there you know." For the past couple of years, I have been using a white ointment on my eyebrows to match my hair and beard. I am really not good with any kind of gels, creams, and things. I cannot even imagine what could happen if I tried to do rosy cheeks! After a long night of appearances at women's and children's shelters, Santa stopped at a local grocery store in his regular civilian clothes to get some microwavable dinner. Santa was having trouble (imagine that!) on the new store self-serve check stand machine. The store attendant came over, curiously looked at me several times, fixed the problem and started to walk away. She turned back around, stared at me again and finally declared, "You do know that your eyebrows are frosted white, right?" Ah, the trials and tribulations of trying to be an authentic Santa Claus.

A little Whiskey never hurt, right?

Earlier I mentioned it is not good to stay in the Santa suit when moving around in public. It is a little hard to stay under the radar for sure. In my years working my regular Marketing job for Casino Resorts, I have always offered my services, during the holiday period, to the sales department staffs to make appearances for them at their Christmas parties on property. It was a nice bonus to the group booked to have Santa make an appearance without any fees involved. At one casino, there were three different properties on the campus. One was across a freeway from the other two, so you needed to drive between them. I did one party at the convention center in one building, then drove across the street to another building. It was a party for Real Estate staff members and their families They were having a rousing good time. I made the rounds of about 250 people. A group of four ladies were having a lot of fun with Santa taking selfies, group photos and lots of teasing. They thought Santa was cute, obviously they all needed glasses! As I finished making my rounds, the catering manager, who was a friend, rushed up and said, "You better make an exit Santa, because the ladies have a spot for you at the bar and already have six shots of whiskey lined up for you." I made my exit as fast as I could. Whew, dodged another bullet. As I was heading out the front door of the western themed casino, I ran into the awesome drummer of the live band that performed every weekend in the lounge. He looked at me a little stunned and said, "Hey Santa, come on back in and I'll buy you a shot." I knew who he was, but he did not know my identity. I thanked him, declined, and headed on my way back to my office to change. That night, the drummer got home and exclaimed to his wife, "You won't believe who I ran into tonight at work. It was Santa, and I offered to buy him some shots." His wife was my boss, smiled and said, "That was Don, from work!" Her husband knew me and could not believe how that all happened. The next week I was suited up again for a few on site holiday events and made arrangements to hand deliver the band's paychecks to them while they were on stage performing. The lounge was packed with guests, including my boss, so Santa danced with everyone. The guests wanted to start buying Santa some shots, so I made my exit, again. I must confess, being an Irishman, it was really hard to pass up a good drink. Oh, the band's name: WHISKEY!

A heavily redacted, classified, stealthy, cloaked in secrecy story!

Sometimes things are just meant to be. Between Thanksgiving and Christmas one year, there had been some horrific and tragic wildfires in the West. Santa was set to travel to a major fire area one year to make appearances at temporary housing centers and fire shelters on Christmas Eve day. I had done it several times before and it was much needed and meaningful to all involved. A week before, I was informed that a local Santa would be able to cover it instead. So, I changed up my schedule and stayed at my home base. Two nights before those Christmas Eve day appearances, that same local Santa came down with a bad virus and would be unable to make the rounds. I got the frantic call to see if I could pull everything back together again at the last minute and travel to the fire area. In checking, it turned out that all of the possible commercial flight routes were sold out in both directions due to the holiday season. The stand-by lists were not looking good as well. The site was also too far to drive back and forth, (six hundred miles each way), as I had numerous Christmas Day appearances as well in my hometown. I talked with the other Santa and told him my dilemma. He was in the military and based in the region of the fire. In talking with him on the phone, something came up that changed everything. It turned out that his base Commander had been the guest speaker at a traveling Vietnam Wall event that I had organized about 8 years earlier. He remembered me and was amazed about the fact that we knew each other and the timing of the whole thing. The base Commander said to the officer, "Let's get it done!" He reached out to the base Commander near where I lived about possible transport to and from the fire area Santa appearances. In the space of 48 hours, it all came together. Another coincidence was the fact that the coordinator of the flights turned out to be my Head Elf at a military base where I had done Santa appearances for many years. What are the chances of that happening? All of the arrangements were made on both ends. I showed up at 0600 (that's 6 AM for you civilians!) on Christmas Eve day to fly to the fire area. My duffle bags, with 2 Santa suits, caused quite a bit of commotion at the base entry gate search to say the least. I was also asked to leave my cell phone in my car as I was not "officially" or "technically" on the flight. Suffice to say this was a very, very big plane. I believe it was called a military transport charter. There was only a dozen or so other passengers. A flight officer stopped by during the flight and asked me, "How you're enjoying the flight you're not on?" I told him that, "If I had been on this flight, it would have been a great flight." I did not mention that I had not received any peanuts yet. After arriving at my destination, I was picked up outside the base and transported to a total of 11 Santa stops at temporary housing shelters in the region before flying home again on a flight that I was "not really on" that night. I got in my car at the base and wrote down dozens of notes about the whole experience. Driving home I thought about how this could only happen to Santa Claus and only on Christmas Eve. The magic of this wonderful time of year had taken over once again. I inquired of my military friend about putting this story in the book and was told that as long as I did not use any staff names, actual base names, any branch of the service names or too much specific information, it "may" be ok. That was enough for me to share it with you! (p.s. mum's the word if you know what I mean). And yes, Santa apparently really does fly, kinda.'

A Look Inside
Volume 1

Kids Say The Darndest Things To Santa Claus: 25 Years of Santa Stories, Volume 1, was a surprise book even to me. I never intended to write it. I've written all my life, but never a book. It happened after 4/5 years of posting annually on Facebook, my favorite Top Ten Humorous and Heartwarming stories after my December volunteer Santa Claus appearances ended. For me it was a way to close out another year, a closure of sorts. For my family and friends, it was a chance to hear about some of my favorite Santa stories after the hustle, bustle of Christmas and New Years had passed. It became such a regular thing that if I got busy in the first few days of the new year and did not post soon enough, I "heard" about it! Each year my family and friends would comment that I, "Needed to write a book." I do not know if anyone just wakes up one day and says, "I'm going to write a book." Plus, I was working full time in a busy, demanding profession. My two days off, like everyone, were filled with errands, appointments, family, and friends, etc. After being hounded long enough, I gave in and started the project.

Wow, what a project it was! I sifted through just over 2, 000 pieces of paper of Santa stories from 25 years. Many cryptic, (my handwriting has always been a tad hard to decipher at best), many unreadable, but most of them manageable. So many humorous and heartwarming stories. For several months I spent 2 to 3 hours a day on each of my days off narrowing down the volume of stories to about six hundred. Then I developed a format for the book which included an explanation of how it all began, the very first time I was Santa and chapters of the locations, (if it was specific to the story), where the stories came from. The locations were important because of the circumstances in which the stories took place. After I had gone through locations, I finished with chapters on behavior and general categories. I was able to put eighty-five stories into the first book. It took me several more months to write all the forwards, lead-ins, and chapters. I wanted to include the best of my recollection of the ages, surroundings, circumstances, environment, and responses. It truly tested my memory. Finally, it and I were done, about 7 months worth of work. Ah yes, but this was just the beginning of phase 2! There's editing, formatting, uploading, downloading, sideloading...

I was fortunate enough to have an amazing, wonderful nephew, Keith James Kennedy, who has an English degree from the University of Wisconsin-Milwaukee and has had three books published so far in his young career. Check out his books under the pen name of Keith JK: *Working Title, Fallen Angel* and *Dreamwalkers.* Keith did the editing and formatting for the book. I am so grateful! I had a lot of other wonderful assistance from friends that are listed in volume 1. BookBaby Publishing was excellent to work with and is a tremendous resource. I highly recommend this great partner.

Prior to and after, once the book and eBook were published, there was lots and lots of sales, marketing, publicity, and social media work to do. I appreciate the advice, counseling, and input from Smith Publicity's Emma Boyer.

The response of readers is what encouraged me to write more. This is volume 2 in the late fall of 2020, and volume 3 will finish out the series in 2022. Altogether, just over six hundred of my favorite Santa stories will be published.

I wanted to share some of the warm, kind, encouraging response I received so far, plus some fun stories as well about the book.

I had to mention the most amazing message of all that I received. It shows just how small our world is after all. Do you know where the island of Malta is? I did not, but I do now. The island is in Europe, just south of Sicily (Italy) in the Mediterranean Sea. The Republic of Malta, an island-state, consists of three islands with a population of 440, 000. I am an author on Goodreads, the top online book review and recommendation website with over ninety million members. On it, readers and authors can communicate, ask questions, get answers, etc. Once readers finish your book, they can simply rate it and/or review it. I received an amazing message in August of 2020 from Albert McCarthy, "I just finished reading your book and gave it five stars. I should know, I actually am the "official" MALTA SANTA Klaws. When you perform something for Charity, the return is greater than cash. Go on Don, more and more children need you." If you Google him, you can read about his journey and life challenges. I was so touched and humbled by his message. It brought me back to why I began doing what I do. Once in a while in life, I believe we need to be reminded of our missions and purpose.

I was blessed to have volume 1 receive a 5-star rating from the book review panel at Readers' Favorites and have included those reviews here.

Just in, as I send this off the publisher, Volume 1 received the Honorable Mention Award at the 2020 International Book Awards for Children - Non-Fiction sponsored by Readers' Favorite. We got edged out for the Bronze Medal by *Meet The Disney Brothers* so we are in good company!

I have also had a great time meeting and communicating with readers on Goodreads and Bookbub and have included many of their comments and reviews as well. Amazon, Barnes & Noble, Google, Apple, Target, Walmart, and others have gotten the book and eBook out there for the world to find and read and it is appreciated. I fondly remember receiving an email right after the eBook was published, Sept. 5, 2019, that the very first reader was from Sydney, Australia! I have truly enjoyed the journey and look forward to beginning volume 3. Stay safe and healthy.

Book Reviews from Readers Favorites review panel:

Liz Konkel – *Kids Say The Darndest Things To Santa Claus by Don Kennedy* is a charming and delightful collection of various moments he has experienced volunteering as Santa Claus. After a friend got sick and he filled in as Santa Claus for a Christmas party, Kennedy found an unexpected passion that would stay with him through the years. Kennedy has gathered together memorable moments from kids that are funny and heartwarming while at times being heartbreaking and eye-opening, taken from his time volunteering for organizations such as fire shelters, hospitals, military bases, and women's shelters. On the surface the book is a simple read that shares quick moments with kids that have made an impact on Don Kennedy when he was Santa, but this also serves as a great eye-opener and reminder about the Christmas spirit and hope that is inspired through these children. Each moment that Kennedy shares is a great example of the role Santa plays in the lives of children. Some moments included are funny while others are touching and will tug at the heart. The humor is delightful in an innocent way such as trying to pay their way off the naughty list, siblings telling on each other, or a boy calling his sister a pain. Kennedy perfectly captures how blunt and innocent kids are through the wonderful and special way they see the world around them. The structure is organized based on the different locations that Kennedy has volunteered at. Each chapter explores various needs the children have from humorous concerns about the naughty list to more heartwarming needs such as wanting their soldier dad to come home. These heartful moments are deeply emotional with kids showing their wit and their heart which include charming moments such as asking Santa to dance with their mom because she's been sad, wanting to visit a man in the hospital who doesn't get visitors, and wanting to send a letter to heaven. Kennedy also shares a few personal stories during his time as Santa such as being pulled over by a cop. Being puked on, getting diet advice, and the touching moments he's been part of, Kennedy's stories are perfect for the holiday season and though it focuses primarily on the Christmas season, *Kids Say The Darndest Things To Santa Claus* is perfect for any time of the year. Each moment spent with the children provides hope and the need to have something special to believe in to get through tough times like deployment, illness, and other difficult situations. The humorous and heartwarming moments will make you smile and warm your heart.

Josh Soule - "Santa has to provide hope, encouragement, comfort, and good cheer for these special families in need." Don Kennedy shares his tale of how he came to be Santa Claus, and some of the interesting experiences with children he encountered along the way. No, this isn't fiction, but when Kennedy's friend, who regularly performed as Santa, came down with a virus, Kennedy has no choice but to step in and take over the responsibility. With the first experience including some challenging questions, blunt comments from children, and even a little vomit, Kennedy found he was a bit more passionate about the role than he thought. From military bases to shelters to hospitals and homes, Santa works his magic with families who needed a bit of Christmas the most. If you read *Kids Say The Darndest Things To*

Santa Claus, I can assure you of three things; you'll laugh, you'll cry, and you'll remember what the spirit of Christmas is all about. With hilarious comments from children such as, "Oh, and if you need help eating all of the cookies that you get, then I'm your man," you'll be sure to laugh out loud as you read. Author Don Kennedy takes it a step further than just a humorous collection of stories and shares the tragic honesty of children experiencing hardship. From reuniting kids with a deployed parent to being asked to deliver a letter to heaven, Kennedy reminds us of what Christmas really means. I found myself touched and inspired to do more this holiday season, and I am grateful to Don Kennedy for sharing *Kids Say The Darndest Things To Santa Claus* with the world.

Donna Gielow McFarland – *Kids Say The Darndest Things To Santa Claus: 25 Years of Santa Stories* by Don Kennedy is a charming collection of stories from Don Kennedy's years as a volunteer Santa Claus. When a friend needed a favor, Kennedy offered to fill in as a substitute Santa, and he had so much fun that he kept it up for 25 years and counting. He volunteers at military bases, fire shelters, Boys & Girls Clubs, and many places where there are children who need compassion and encouragement. What makes Kennedy a little unique is that from the very beginning, after each Santa event, he had the presence of mind to write down things the kids said to him. *Kids Say The Darndest Things To Santa Claus* is a collection of these special stories with additions about what goes on behind the scenes. Additions like what happens when Santa gets pulled over by a police officer... Don Kennedy's stories range from comical to heart-wrenching. Many of the children in the stories are similar age – about seven years old – but they have a wide range of concerns. Dad shot a deer – was it one of the reindeer? Can you please do something about my little brother? Our house burned down so we can't bake cookies, is that okay? Boys, particularly, are worried about being on the naughty list.

There are kids who hilariously embarrass their parents. There are kids worried about parents on military assignments overseas and kids from third world countries who want Santa to bring food or shoes to their friends back home. One of my favorites was the kid who was desperate to hitch a ride on the sleigh because he needed to be in the 'witness 'tection program' because Sarah wanted to kiss him! The stories are probably better suited for adult readers than for children. It is totally, completely heartwarming. Read it during the holidays, with a hot mug of cocoa or in front of a crackling fire, and at a time when there is someone else at home to whom you can read aloud your favorite stories.

Gisela Dixon – *Kids Say The Darndest Things To Santa Claus: 25 Years of Santa Stories* by Don Kennedy is a short non-fiction memoir about Don's experiences as a volunteer Santa Claus for organizations that cannot afford to hire a "professional" Santa during the Christmas holiday season. In this book, Don describes how he got started on this gig when he filled in as Santa Claus for someone who couldn't make it. Through this, he realized he enjoyed it and developed a passion for it, especially at places where he could volunteer his services for free such as charity organizations, non-profit foundations, etc. The book is organized into chapters which detail Don's experiences with children at fire shelters, hospitals, children's centers, women's shelters, military bases, and such. There is also a short author bio at the end of the book. *Kids Say The Darndest Things To Santa Claus* is an entertaining book that describes the various things that kids say to Santa Claus, some of which are funny and amusing and range from simple things to lavish ones. There are sometimes also cases of abused or neglected children that express things to Santa which are disturbing, and Don rightly informs the organizers and social services when there is any hint of abuse. Don writes in a basic, straightforward style that simply describes the child's wishes and dreams. His passion for this volunteer work which he has been doing for 25 years comes through strongly in the book. Overall, this is a collection of fun and entertaining anecdotes of what kids ask for or say to Santa Claus.

Sarah Stuart – *Kids Say The Darndest Things To Santa Claus: 25 Years of Santa Stories* by Don Kennedy is a collection of ten chapters of true stories about how this Santa handled playing his part. He is right that being Santa at events, or special places, is very different from seeing children briefly in a mall Booth - "a quick hello, what's your name & age, what is your wish for Christmas, smile for the photo, and done" - as Don Kennedy puts it. The comedy comes mainly from fast answers to potentially awkward responses. "Story" does not always indicate a merry tale; there's a serious side to each chapter. Given time, children confide in the man in the red suit with the fluffy beard, and his response can change lives, especially when he picks up on abuse and takes action. I was hooked by the first chapter, "The Military," and in tears over the boy who "didn't talk about Daddy cos it made Mommy cry." Shocked by "Shelters" and the security surrounding them – even Santa isn't told their location until he arrives accompanied by the staff! There is laugh-aloud comedy too. In "Young Love," Santa is asked to marry two six-year-olds "before our mommies get back." "Siblings" features rivalry, including a girl who begs a ride on the sleigh for her brother, so Santa can dump him on Mars. Every reader will have their favorites. *Kids Say The Darndest Things To Santa Claus* by Don Kennedy is a winner that would make a super Christmas gift.

What other readers had to share:

Sharen Schermer – A very special Christmas present! My family & friends loved this book!!! It brought tears & laughter to many this Christmas!!! (OK, I fess up, she is my first cousin and fellow middle child in her family, and she does have very good taste none-the- less!)

J. Mucceli – This is a great little, short read recommended for all children & adults. All will enjoy this heartwarming book, some very hilarious moments, be ready to laugh. This is for the paperback given to me and kindly signed by Santa Don.

Nicole Woods – This is such a fantastic book. I couldn't stop smiling as I read all of the wonderful stories and also found myself getting choked up as well. I enjoyed getting to view real life stories through the lens of Santa, some heartwarming, some emotional and some were just downright hysterical. This is such a great book, and I would recommend it to all of my family & friends.

Ezra – Dear Santa Don, Thank you so much for this book. I wanted it as soon as I saw it. It just seems so funny. I will have a lot of laughs from it. Sincerely, Ezra (a student of a great friend of mine from New Mexico)

Lori Tatar – This sweet book is charming, heartfelt & heart-warming. Told with a kind and gentle voice, these stories will just plain make you feel good and can be shared with elves of all ages, large and small.

Kathleen Conrad – Kids do say the best things. I really enjoyed this read. It was fun and sweet and with my daughter all grown, it brought me back to younger days.

Pat Doucett – This book is a charming and delightful read. I would give it ten stars if they were available. Santa Don obviously has a big heart when it comes to kids. There were laughs because kids are so ingenious when it comes to talking their way out of tough situations, but there were also tears when you read some of their sad stories. Situations that children that age shouldn't have to be exposed to, but nobody said life will be easy at any age. I personally want to thank Santa Don for your kindness to all these children because they certainly deserved it. I highly recommend this book. I know you will enjoy it as much as I did.

Amy – Thanks Santa Don for coming out to Sandy Valley, Nevada to meet us and sign your book. It's the first and maybe the only time I ever met an author. I loved the book and have shared it with many people. Also, thanks for donating all the proceeds to the youth in our community. Keep up the great work!

Gail – This book can be read at one sitting or small dosages. It was a great way to kick off the holiday season a little early. My 11-year-old daughter also read it and enjoyed it quite a bit. A cute book to reflect about what you have and giving to others.

Dawn Kieser – I read it from cover to cover in the first hour after it arrived. I found myself laughing, crying, and sometimes whispering a prayer as I read each section. The stories were funny, sad, silly, and touching as the author detailed 25 years of stories kids told to Santa. I recommend this book for anyone who loves kids and enjoys the adorable things they say.

Tanya – A fun compilation of stories and experiences from Santa. I enjoyed hearing about how impactful a friendly Santa face can be to kids of all ages, and it was also a great reminder to be grateful for all I have in life. This book will be a great addition to my other Christmas coffee table books. Its bite sized and can be read a little at a time or all at once.

Esther Smith – Super adorable, this book really has started getting me into the holiday spirit. WOW, kids definitely say some crazy things. I loved the author's background!

Emile Graham – This was a very sweet book! It's a fast and feel-good read, it was fun.

Robin Black – It's a feel-good book and I applaud Mr. Kennedy for volunteering his time to be with all these kids at Christmas!

Stephanie – Absolutely love! Very clever and fun read. Thanks Santa Don!

Ella James – This is a wonderful, fun book. I totally enjoyed it and highly recommend it!

Mary Ann – Santa DON! Thanks so much for coming to Lincoln City, Oregon to sign books and give back the proceeds to our community charities!

Paige Okamura - Kumu Olelo Hawaii, UH Manoa– Aloha and mahalo nui for your leka and makana. Ke Aloha Nui!

During the pandemic, I heard, as we all did, of all of the health care professionals and first responders overwhelmed at times and so I donated three signed books to every hospital in the state of Hawaii plus Police and Fire departments on the Waianae Coast of Oahu to read, escape and enjoy some fun stories. Here's a few responses I received.

Judith V. Teves – Director of Nursing – Critical Access, Lanai Community Hospital – Aloha Don, we received the copies of your authored books for our staff during this pandemic. We appreciate your sharing it with us. Godspeed in all your writing endeavors. Mahalo

Lori Suan, MPH Director of Development, Shriners Hospitals for Children at Honolulu – Thank you so much for your generous gift of three autographed copies of your book for our staff and patients. It is important to us that you know how grateful we are for the support and encouragement you continue to give our young patients and their families. Mahalo for being part of our Shriners Hospitals 'Ohana! Please know that our patients, families, and organization appreciate you.

I did some book signings after the book was published. It was a lot of fun interacting with readers and the public. I did a number of bookstores, cruise ships plus places like Lincoln City and

Portland, Oregon; Sandy Valley and Reno/Lake Tahoe, Nevada and more. Here's are few responses as well.

Captain Christopher B. Lye, Master – MV Star Princess – Thank you very much for joining us on our Hawaiian cruise and your onboard book events plus copies for our ship's library. My wife Jenny and I are looking forward to reading it. My favorite books are mostly with a connection to the sea of some sort. I don't recall ever having read a "Christmas" book and am looking forward to it as a complete change very much! Once again, an enormous thank you for your kindness.

Gary Kelly – Chairman of the Board & Chief Executive Officer – Southwest Airlines – Thank you for sending an autographed copy of your new book plus giving one to both of our flight crews on your first book tour from Las Vegas to Portland, Oregon and back. I'm sure they were delighted. I look forward to reading it and sharing it with my family. We LUV having "Santa Don" onboard our flights!

OK, that's all about Volume 1.

A Look Inside Volume 2

You finally write your first book. It was a true labor of love. They said it could never be done (me too!). It takes 7 months in all to pull it all together. It gets published so now you can sit back and move on to other challenges in life, right. Wrong. The response to book 1 of *Kids Say The Darndest Things To Santa Claus* was so positive and full of encouragement from family, friends, and readers, I had to seriously think about writing more. People whom I had never met were so appreciative of the project that I felt I should keep going. Plus, I had hundreds of additional stories to tell. Also, there was year 26 & 27 of being Santa which added even more material to share. So, I did keep writing and book 2 came to be. It's also what encouraged me to write this book, volume 3.

I am very honored and appreciative of several recognitions of book 2 which were received. First was a Five Star Book Review from the review panel at Readers Favorite. The second was the International Finalist Book Excellence Award in Non-Fiction from the Literary Excellence Awards LLC. The third was the Silver Award for Humor from the Kops Fetherling International Book Awards. I didn't write these books for any recognition, so it is really humbling to receive these.

One of the biggest surprises to me is that the books are being read by children. I wrote the books for adults, mainly parents, grandparents, organizers of children's holiday events and Elves. However, between people reading the books to their children, librarians reading them at events, and teachers reading the books to their classes, kids are picking them up on their own. Wow, you never know what can happen when it comes to books and eBooks. Lots of children sent messages to me, and I'll share a few here: from Melody, "I can't believe I said the same things that kids do in your two books!" From Mason, "Wow, I remember saying all the same funny and silly stuff in the book, no wonder my grandparents used to laugh so hard when they took me to see Santa Claus." Anthony added, "Oh no, I must have really been a dork at Christmas time. How do you not laugh out loud at us kids Santa!!!" Very special to me was a letter from my great nephew Braden who wrote, "Dear Uncle Don/Santa, I loved your books, they are funny. My number one story in your books is the kid that asked for a cool hairdo and a hot girlfriend." And super special from my great niece Emery who wrote, Dear Uncle Don, Grandpa K (my brother Jim) reads stories from your volume 2 book to me. I liked the stories! Love, Emery."

Volume 2 received a bunch of reviews from Readers Favorite, Goodreads, Library Thing, Entrada Publishing and more. I've shared a number of them here.

Reviewed by K.C. Finn for Readers' Favorite - Kids Say the Darndest Things to Santa Claus Volume 2: 25 Years of Santa Stories is a work of non-fiction in the comedy, holiday reading, and true to life sub-genres, and was penned by author Don Kennedy. This is the second book in the series and consists of anecdotes about the author's experience of volunteering as Santa Claus for over 25 years. The stories within this collection concern children in a wide range of circumstances and vary from the hilarious to the heartbreaking to the heartwarming. A charming narrative and wonderful insight into what Christmas can mean to children everywhere, both the hope it brings as well as the excitement. Author Don Kennedy really knows how to deliver a holiday text that will warm even the deepest recesses of the hardest hearts during this Christmas season. I was fascinated to step into a perspective that I'd never really thought about before, and experience a secret world of young children and their fondest wishes, whispered to a figure they trust and believe in. The work is beautifully presented and always easy to pick up for a beautiful, emotional moment, and I also loved the fact that Santa Don didn't shy away from some of the more pressing issues and harrowing circumstances that some kids go through. This is a work which really illustrates the magic of hope, and how Christmas can be a conduit to hope for a better future. Overall, I would highly recommend Kids Say the Darndest Things to Santa Claus Volume 2: 25 Years of Santa Stories for anyone looking for a charming stocking filler this holiday season.

Reviewed by Susan Sewell for Readers' Favorite - Discover the joys and pains of the Season of Miracles in the laugh out-loud book, Kids Say the Darndest Things to Santa Claus (25 Years of Santa Stories, Volume 2) by Don Kennedy. Is there a better way to start celebrating Christmas than to visit Santa Claus? Follow a volunteer Santa as he travels the world (and maybe the heavens) to meet precocious little ones anxious to talk to Santa. This Santa has been everywhere, and just when he thinks he's heard everything, the next child to sit on his lap delivers another priceless gem. Learn what every soldier needs for success according to a six-year-old, how to deal with unruly siblings, and what Mom's new diet can mean for poor Santa Claus this Christmas Eve in this enchanting book. Move over Art Linkletter and make room for Santa Don! But be warned, he's telling all in the humorous and heartwarming collection of amusing stories in Kids Say the Darndest Things to Santa Claus. Get in the holiday spirit with the most disarming and endearing anecdotes from adorable children aged from three to nine. Delightful and disarming, the honesty and guilelessness of the children speaking to Santa were both entertaining and fun to read. I enjoyed this book! It is beautifully balanced between moving and delightful anecdotes; I laughed, I cried, then laughed some more! I enjoyed the sometimes-brutal honesty of the children and appreciated Don Kennedy's dedication and foresight to record and share some of his most memorable moments as a volunteer in shelters, hospitals, military bases, churches, etc. The second book in a series of three, this volume will not disappoint!

Reviewed by Gail Kamer for Readers' Favorite - In Kids Say the Darndest Things to Santa Claus: 25 Years of Santa Stories, Volume 2, author Don Kennedy shares stories about what kids have told him while making a visit to Santa Claus, AKA Don Kennedy. Don has volunteered as a Santa in a variety of settings and with each one, the experience is unique, fun, and often heartrending. Stories about Christmas wishes, and family secrets make for a quick and fun read. In addition to the Santa visits, Don provides advice to current or would-be Santa's. I laughed and cried while reading Kids Say the Darndest Things to Santa Claus. Don Kennedy's tricks of the trade as an experienced Santa are invaluable to any Santa and, indeed, to anyone who works with children or adults. His understanding of giving hope without making unrealistic promises provides ideas for anyone in a difficult situation. Kids Say the Darndest Things to Santa Claus is an asset I wish I had access to while in this role. In addition to Don's sage knowledge, I found myself thinking of practical application of his wisdom and his stories. Are you working on a newsletter for your staff for the holidays? Are you preparing a speech for your holiday celebration? You'll find great tidbits here to add to it. Or do you just need to put a smile on your face and remember what the true meaning of Christmas is? Kids Say the Darndest Things to Santa Claus would make a great addition to your library, no matter the purpose.

Rachel Smith for Entrada Publishing Book Reviews - Kids Say the Darndest Things to Santa Claus Volume 2 Review - Volunteer Santa turned author Don Kennedy is back with the second installment in his three-book series describing his adventures over the past 25 years. Kids Say the Darndest Things to Santa Clause Volume 2 is a heart-warming and occasionally humorous collection of short stories chronicling his experiences with children and adults. If you missed the first volume don't worry, Don Kennedy has included a helpful introduction at the start of the book. Readers new to the series won't have any problems following along as Don Kennedy makes appearances as Santa Claus. He does warn readers familiar with the first book that some of the stories in the second one are repeats, but the majority are new for everyone. Once again, Don Kennedy has made it easy to keep his visits straight. Each chapter deals with a specific volunteer visit. The author shows readers the importance of Santa Claus in children's lives, especially when times are hard. Whether it's at a military base, a shelter for women and children, or a hospital, the author gives readers a touching account of his visits. There is also a message for adults in Kids Say the Darndest Things to Santa Claus Volume 2. It reminds readers that kids are perceptive and resilient. Children also need hope. This is what Don Kennedy brings to children every time he puts his Santa suit on. Like the first volume, readers will find plenty of humor in the book. Young love, siblings, questions, and jokes told by kids have also made it into the second volume. "A few kids later, a little girl came up, stared at Santa, and blurted out, "You better drink skim milk or 2% milk cause you look really fat!" Her mother was horrified but I told her that Mrs. Claus had me on a new diet. She seemed satisfied with that. Kids do say the darndest things to Santa Claus and now he's telling all in his second volume in time for the holidays.

Kathy Henkins Goodreads Review - Who doesn't want to read something sweet and funny right now? We all need whatever help we can get to put a smile on our faces, I think. You can't go wrong by reading Don Kennedy's Kids Say the Darndest Things to Santa Claus. I heartily enjoyed the second volume of a trilogy, this one containing over 200 sometimes sweet, sometimes hilarious, almost always heart-warming (and occasionally saddening) entries. Kennedy's first volume of Kids Say was published in 2019 following the great interest shown in his Santa experiences described on his Facebook page. Kennedy was a volunteer Santa for 25 years, appearing for several hours each time – unlike the few minutes a Santa is able to give children at shopping malls. In the introduction, he explains that he appeared as Santa for charities and organizations that could not afford to pay for a visit. He recounts stories collected from Boys and Girls Clubs, hospitals, military bases, women's and children's shelters, schools, churches, and the like. This volume separates the funny things kids say into categories like Parents and Grandparents, Siblings, The Naughty List and The Doubters. There is a chapter centered on the joke's children tell Santa and one featuring the many "couples" who want to inform Santa about their plans to be "marriaged." I could never have imagined how honest, forthright, and unfiltered the kids were. Kennedy records their comments about how fat Santa has become – "I'm thinking you might want to try the air vent" because he might otherwise get stuck in the chimney, for example. They ask whether Rudolph's nose is red for the same reason their uncle's is, drinking a lot. And one child tells Santa that if he ever gets divorced from Mrs. Claus, "my Nana's quite a catch." Knowing that Kennedy has freely given his time for so many years, it makes sense that he, unknowingly, shows us his creativity and deep compassion – evident in his part of the many conversations. He is respectful with every child; he has the rare ability to recognize what children are really saying, what they need to hear, what will make the most sense or will help the most. I expected the laugh and smile while reading this book, but I didn't expect to be so touched at the same time. I plan to acquire the 3rd volume soon. It doesn't have to be Christmas to derive joy from kids and Santa Claus.

Keahi Kahale Goodreads Review - I was glad that the author wrote a second book with more stories. I found myself putting it down, then picking it up again just to smile. I think one thing I enjoy is recalling my times with Santa Claus as a child. The author captures that really well. I like that sometimes he comments or goes further with stories, and some are just what the kids say. I'm going to get some books and use as Christmas presents for people, I know that like to read. I also like that not every story is funny and silly. There's lots of more heartwarming and heartfelt stories as well. The chapter on the doubting kids is funny too because many are not 100% sure that they are past the Santa period but also afraid of being wrong! I enjoyed there being so many more stories than the first book. I'm intrigued by the author's background and career too. Please keep writing that 3rd book because I'm not filled up yet Santa Don!!! I would also like to read about being a Santa during the Covid-19 period in our lives. All in all, I really enjoyed the book. It's a fun and heartwarming read. Perfect for the holidays for sure.

Dawn Davis Goodreads Review - As a former teacher, I really wish I had written down and saved all of the wonderful, fun, and silly things my students did and said! This book captured the innocence, brutal honesty, heartwarming comments, and cute interactions perfectly. I was taken by what all goes into being Santa Claus. I had never given much thought to what all is involved. Just the "suiting up" and dressing back into "civies" sounds like a real time-consuming process. I also was taken by all the various locations Santa goes to. I initially thought this book would be about Santa's at shopping malls. Reading this brought laughter, tears, and every emotion in between. It could have been just a book of all happy moments but that's not what life is for all of us no matter what age. I felt like Santa Don let us into the wonderful, magical yet often tragic world of children at Christmas time. Seeing and experiencing this world through his eyes and ears was a rare treat. I always enjoyed Art Linkletter and his interactions with children both on TV and in his books. This is just as special. I'm going back now to read the first volume. I did like the way Santa Don set up his readers of volume 2 in case they had not read book 1. It was very thoughtful of him for the reader. THANKS SANTA DON!

Debra Jeakins Goodreads Review - KIDS SAY THE DARNDEST THINGS TO SANTA CLAUS VOLUME #2 BY DON KENNEDY. Mr. Kennedy is a volunteer Santa, which means he gets no money to travel to various places like military bases/hospitals/shelters and charges ZERO for his time and service. Mr. Kennedy's reward? The stories of the children he has met with and brought happiness to. Some of these often humorous and sometimes tear-jerking stories are compiled in the second of his books.

With this book, as well as the first volume, Mr. Kennedy has brought the real meaning of Christmas back to me. The love, comfort and yes, the time spent doing Santa for nothing, but the joy Mr. Kennedy has brought to children's lives who need it more than ever. You will laugh but I myself could not help but cry at some of the stories. Well worth the time to read, whether it's Christmas Day or the middle of the summer!

Michelle Goodreads Review - One man's accounts of what playing Santa is all about. We all need to believe in something, and the magic of Christmas truly outshines itself. Just the lights on the trees and the music lift our spirits. Kids say the darndest things all year but confiding in Santa, they sometimes just say it like it is. To be the one listening and having to contain yourself sounds very hard. I'm glad that you shared your stories with us.

Betty Goodreads Review - This book was so funny! I love the way the author preserved the honest words from the mouths of babes.

Glenn Stenquist Goodreads Review - Anyone who likes kids and the honesty that comes from them will enjoy this book and likely pass it on.

Love those kids! By BG Knighton, Amazon book reviews – A delightful book of anecdotes from Don's years as a Santa. Kids do say the darndest things! Very enjoyable. (If you like these stories, please check out Art Linkletter's books.)

Charity R.B. Howard, Amazon book reviews. – This is well-written with sweet, heartwarming, and fun stories!

Review by Jenn Ray from Reedsy Discovery book website: If you want something to read to your kids or compare your kids' stories to these, then this is a book for you.

Kids Say The Darndest Things to Santa Claus reads exactly as the title intends. The author, Don Kennedy, spent 25 years working as a Santa Claus for various events and, over the years, collected an array of stories from his time as the icon. Some are sad, some are heartfelt, but most are just silly as you would expect from young children.

For a wholesome, fun Christmas read for the family, I recommend Kids Say The Darndest Things to Santa Claus Volume 2 by Don Kennedy.

As with Volume 1, the second book was published during the pandemic period. I provided copies of the book to hospitals, emergency departments and other care providers on all of the Hawaiian Islands. I'm sharing two of those thank you letters here.

From Janice N. Knapp, CFRE Director of Development for Shriners Hospitals for Children in Honolulu, "Dear Mr. Kennedy, thank you so much for your generous gift of three signed copies of your book, Kids Say The Darndest Things To Santa Claus Volume 2 as you did with Volume 1. Shriners Hospital for Children improves the lives of children by providing pediatric specialty care, conducting innovative research, and offering outstanding educational programs for medical professionals. Children up to age 18 with orthopaedical conditions are eligible for care, regardless of the families' ability to pay, and receive care and services in a compassionate family-centered environment. Mahalo for being part of our Shriners Hospitals for Children 'Ohana! Please know that our patients, families, and organization appreciate you. From Kanoe Paauhau, Director of House Operations for Ronald McDonald House of Hawaii, "Aloha Don Kennedy. On behalf of the staff, families, and especially the children of Ronald McDonald House in Honolulu, I would like to extend a special Mahalo for your generous in-kind donation of "Kids Say The Darndest Things To Santa Claus" Volumes 1 & 2. You are making a difference in the lives of families as they fortify their strength to meet the demands of battling their children's' illness. Your commitment to the House and our mission allows us to provide accommodations, meals, Wi-Fi, transportation, and other vital services. Ronald McDonald House serviced nearly 29, 300 men, women, and children since opening our doors here in 1987. We strive to provide a "home-away-from-home" for our special families, and this is only made possible through the warm support and donations from the community. We are deeply grateful for your caring. Please accept our warmest best wishes from the "House That Love Built."

From Santa's mailbox, some more fun notes. From lifelong friend and former co-worker Peggi Sanders, "my nieces and nephews love these stories, and it reminds them of the dumb things they said to Santa when they were smaller. I have a great quote for your book. When Randy was 5, now 29, he told me that he knew how Santa got to all the kids on Christmas Eve. He said when Santa left the North Pole, he froze time and when he returned, he just turned time back on. I thought it was pretty good for a 5-year-old."

From Mary Ellen of a Hawaiian women's & children's shelter, "thanks so much for the wonderful donation of your two books as well as your visits these past two years. With the pandemic, everyone is a little hesitant to come forward with support. With Mahalos and Aloha Santa!"

From Claudia & Steve Quan, "Dear Don, just a note of thanks for giving us your book. We read through it with tears in our eyes… how you handle yourself thru it all was amazing." From Ellen & Robert N. in Maui, "thanks so much for providing copies of your books for our fundraiser programs here on the island. It was the hit of the night as we enter the holiday season. God speed on your travels all over the islands next month." From Sarah & Jason of Hilo, "Mele Kalikimaka and Mahalo Nui Loa for the wonderful donation of your books for our big event raising funds for the keikis in need programs on our big island." From Iolani & Keahi, "Mahalo Santa Don for coming to Kuaui and also donating the books for our program, the Garden Isle truly appreciates your kokua and wishes you Aloha!" From Chrystal & David Tuckness, "Thank you so much for the book! What a roller coaster of emotions. Thank you for sharing. God bless."

Some more from Santa's mailbag. From Mia and Kahiau, "Mahalo Nui Santa Don for your visit to Kailua, not sure who enjoyed it more, the Tutu's and Papa's or the Keiki!!! Safe travels please as your sleigh makes its way around our beloved Hawaii Nei." From Brenda and Kai of Kahuku, "Dear Santa Don, so very appreciative on behalf of everyone, especially with the covid outbreak, that you came to visit us this holiday season. Be safe, be happy and come back next year, PLEASE!" From Kule'a and K.C. of Ewa, "Aloha Santa. Much Mahalos for coming to be with all of the Keiki in our Ewa Beach. Everyone had a lovely time and it brightened all of the faces of our Kupuna (seniors) too." From Christine and Eric in Haleiwa, "Mahalo Nui Uncle Don for coming to be Santa for our keiki. Everybody was so surprised to see the REAL Santa Claus in person. WOW!!! Please be healthy and stay safe this year. Aloha!"

Just a few more so I don't leave anyone out! From Leilani and Aaron of Haleiwa, "Mahalo, Mahalo and more Mahalos from all of us at the church. Can we sign Santa up again for 2022?? We can't wait till next time. All of the keiki loved their candy canes. OK, so did some of the adults in the room too! Does Santa surf 'cause we've got the best surfing here on the North Shore. Santa seen shredding, that would be so EPIC!!!" From Kailani and Jared of Wahiawa, "our entire organization here wants to say MAHALO for coming to be our Santa for all of our keiki. We couldn't have dreamed for anything better than what you brought to us. Please be safe and healthy and take our sincere blessings with you in your journeys."

From the Makaha Valley Plantation monthly newsletter: Hau'oli Makahiki Hou! Happy New Year!

"Thanks to everyone who came to our Meet Santa event in December! Dozens of families and hundreds of keiki got to meet the man in red, and our sincere thanks to Don Kennedy for volunteering his Santa-services. Please go to www.makaha-valleyplantation.org/community to see our day with Santa. Also, this feel-good story will be in the February issue of the regional community newspaper, "Westside Stories"!

Special thanks to our Santa: Donald Kennedy, Santa's elves, MVP office and security team, Andrew Clark, Jane Finstrom, Grey Schmidt, Bonzai, and to Susana Poulin for the use of her Sleigh.

Thank you also to Aunty Pattie for pitching in when she saw we needed help gathering names for the raffle."

Whenever I get to cruise the great high seas, I always get a copy of the books to the Captain, Cruise Director, stateroom steward, server staff as well as for the ship Library. Here's a few notes from the ship Captains: Captain Steve MacBeath of the Holland America Line's Koningsdam, "Dear Don, thank you for the copy of your book, as a father to two boys, it is definitely an entertaining read and quite a journey you embarked on. Thanks for the copies for our Library as well. I do hope you enjoy your time onboard. Safe travels." Captain Karl Staffan Bengtsson of the Norwegian Cruise Line Bliss, "thank you for copies of your two books, greatly appreciated. I'm certain all of the book and eBook readers on board will truly enjoy them." From Captain Luca Lazzarino of the Carnival Panorama, "what a delightful surprise, thank you. All of us on the bridge will love reading the books." From Captain Dino Sagani of the M/V Majestic Princess, "Dear Santa Don, I am delighted that you have chosen to sail with us aboard the Majestic Princess and hope you are enjoying a wonderful time. I received your kind gift of the book and will like to take this opportunity to thank you for the book and kind thought. As well for our Library. It is a pleasure sailing with you. I look forward to hosting you again on any Princess ship that I will command in the future. Kind regards."

So that's a look inside Volume 2, hope you enjoyed it.

Meet the Author
DON KENNEDY

Don Kennedy is a resident of Makaha Valley on Oahu, Hawaii. He's a longtime resident of Nevada: Las Vegas, Lake Tahoe & Reno. Over his life, he's lived in thirteen cities in nine states. He's a third-time author or as the infamous W.C. Fields referred to writers, "scrivener." He's a member of the Hawaii Writer's Guild. Kennedy began writing as editor of his high school newspaper plus sports reporter for his local community newspaper and has continued ever since. His first book: *Kids Say The Darndest Things To Santa Claus: 25 Years of Santa Stories* was published in fall of 2019 in eBook and paperback. His second book by the same title, Volume 2, was published in fall 2020. Volume 3 is being published in fall of 2022. All are available online through all major retailers.

Born and raised in Wisconsin, Kennedy is a graduate of Concordia College where he studied for the ministry. He worked as a staff assistant to the Lieutenant Governor of Wisconsin Martin J. Schreiber and served a 4-year term as an elected member of the Milwaukee County Board of Supervisors. He was appointed as a Congressional Page in the U.S. House of Representatives for Foreign Relations Committee Chairman Congressman Clement J. Zablocki in Washington D.C. while in high school. He has been involved in numerous community and charitable organizations.

He was a radio and TV broadcaster and print editor/publisher for more than a decade. Kennedy was a city editor and sports editor for the *Henderson Home News* and *Boulder City News*, reporter for the *Pahrump Valley Times*, editor of *Vegarama, Las Vegas Top Spots, Las Vegas Sports News* and *Las Vegas Pizazz* magazine, publisher/editor of *Going Places/Southwest Traveler* magazine, and feature writer for Valley Electric's *Ruralite* magazine. He was a radio personality on KVOV and KREL radio stations plus hosted a syndicated travel radio program, "Going Places," on the local NBC Talk Radio station. He provided voice-overs and commercial broadcasting on several TV stations including KVVU TV 5.

For 35 years, Kennedy was a casino marketing executive with titles of manager, director, vice president, corporate vice president, AGM and CMO in seven states: Nevada, California, Oregon, New Mexico, Louisiana, Indiana, and Oklahoma. He has served as a judge for the prestigious Romero Awards for a decade, plus been a guest speaker/lecturer at numerous seminars, conferences, conventions, and several universities. A Roast/Toast celebrating his career was held in 2015 and is available on You Tube titled: "Don Kennedy Roast Primm 2015." He's received many awards and honors in his careers.

Kennedy enjoys travel, especially where there are lakes and oceans. He is semi-retired in Hawaii. He has been an active member and officer of the NFL Alumni Association for 20 years as an Associate Member. He's a proud uncle to two nieces, a nephew, grandniece, and grandnephew, and has two brothers. Twice married, he has no children.

Kennedy's nickname is, "The Phantom," given to him by mentor and renowned casino marketing guru John Romero because no one could keep track of him with his casino hospitality career constantly moving him around the country. Where he would land, nobody knew. His new nickname is "Makaha," the story of how it came to be is revealed in Volume 3.

His passion, every December for the past 25 years, has been serving as a volunteer Santa Claus for all those who needed to be seen, heard, and given a little Christmas spirit. Don believes in "giving back."

Very Special Dedications

Special Dedications to Joel A. Leong, Kenny Davis, Jackie Brett, John Romero, Mualeava Lene, Gilbert "ZuLu" Kauhi, Herman Wedemeyer, plus my Hawaiian 'Ohana

One unique opportunity that is afforded to an author is make special dedications in their books to honor and recognize people in their lives who have made meaningful, wonderful, and lasting impressions. In my first book, I recognized dozens of parents, grandparents, and family members whom I considered role models of parenting and family. In my second book I dedicated it to my close friend Richard P. Mirabal and my older brother and hero James F. Kennedy. I have been blessed and so fortunate in my life to meet and make lifelong friends with the very best of humanity. In this, my third book, I am recognizing and making dedication to seven individuals and one very special group. Plus three tributes of those who have gone before us. Please bear with me, as you will see that my dedications are not just a few paragraphs, but full stories filled with all kinds of memories, insights, and tributes.

Joel Akana Leong, "Bruddah Joel," "Joey," my personal "Professor & Kumu" and "Papa" to his grandchildren, is one of those folks you meet along your path in life and instantly want to be friends with. A lifelong resident of Honolulu on the island of Oahu, Hawaii, Joel was a graduate of the University of Hawaii at Manoa. I met Joel some 33 years ago at this writing when I was Vice President of Marketing for the High Sierra/Horizon Casino Resort (Sahara Tahoe) in Lake Tahoe, Nevada on the California border. Joel was part of the family business of Creative Holidays, Cruise Holidays Hawaii & TRU, Travel Resources Unlimited, a Hawaiian travel agency and wholesale tour company. Key principals in the company were wife Lissa (Lum), sister-in-law Didi Ah Yo (Lum), brother-in-law Paul Ah Yo, brother-in-law Preston Lum and close family friend Marmie Kaaihue. Hawaiians love to snow ski and snowboard and they loved coming to the Sierra mountains with its sixteen ski resorts surrounding Lake Tahoe. Islanders also love to gamble, so the casinos were another attraction. Spring Break in March was a key travel period. I worked closely with the travel company for a decade while in Lake Tahoe and Reno. I would visit the islands twice each year, hosting dinner parties for travel agents, airline sales staffs and casino players. However, as the years went on, a business relationship turned into a real friendship, a true bond. The Lum, Ah Yo and Leong families annually hosted a backyard Luau and pre/post parking lot tailgate for the NFL Pro Bowl. I attended the Pro Bowl and events fifteen times. I became Ohana (family). When I moved to Hawaii, Joel and I became closer. I joined in family dinners, attended Hawaiian language Olelo classes with him at the University of Hawaii Manoa, attended holiday and sports events and portrayed Santa Claus for his grandchildren. He also taught me "pidgin" which is the unofficial third language of Hawaii, behind the Hawaiian and English languages. Actually "pidgin" may be the #2 language! I had asked Joel to help me with pidgin when I just could not figure out what my Makaha Hawaiian neighbor was saying to me each time I left to go to Honolulu. It turned out he was saying "shoots," or "shootz" which means "OK, see you, cool, sounds good." My neighbor also told me since I lived on the Waianae Coast, it may be better to learn the pidgin words and phrases rather than the full Hawaiian language! Joel was only too happy to teach me. A few other examples of that special language: "Eh, howzit?" which means, "Hey, how's it going?" And "Cannah talk da kine?" which means, "Can't you speak pidgin?" Another, "Eh, what school you went?" meaning the school you attended. My favorite cashier at the Waianae L & L restaurant was thrilled when I said "shoots" one day and declared, "Uncle Don, you so local now!" Actually, at first, I thought she said I was "loco," which would also be true. But I digress.

I consider Joel an absolute treasure of a person, an amazing husband, father, brother, and grandfather. I am so very happy, blessed, and fortunate to know him. Joel passed in December of 2021. We were just beginning to plan my second year of being Santa for his grandchildren or "moopuna." And yes, it went on as planned. There are two other stories about Joel in other sections of this book, so, I will not repeat them here. One is in the chapter, "Yes, Virginia, Santa Really Does Know Hawaiian," which includes how I got my Hawaiian nickname and the other in, "It Can Only Happen to Santa," all about my first Santa visit with Joel's family.

Joels immediate family includes wife Lissa, son Kala'e and Beth, and son Ryan and Iolani plus children Kahiau, Ku'lea and Kupa'a. He has one brother and four sisters, two surviving, Joleen "Sweetie" Leong Yamaguchi, husband Myles, and Jonia "Queenie" Leong Kamada, husband Glenn, and lots of nieces, nephews, and cousins. He loved them all dearly.

"A hui hou Bruddah Joel, A hui hou!" (Until we meet again.)

Kenneth "Kenny Bob" Davis, veteran actor, comedian, musician, singer, and "lifeguard," as he would remind his audiences, could have been my brother. He was the opening comedy performer for a decade with The Gatlin Brothers and opened for headliners like

Kenny Rogers, Willie Nelson, Vince Gill and even the immortal George Burns. He was in many movies including Gremlins and on hit TV shows including "ER," where he played the part of a drunken Santa! In real life, he was the absolute best Santa Claus ever. I learned quite a bit about how to portray Santa from my mentor Kenny Bob. I met Kenny in 1989 when he literally "saved my life!" He was the comedy star in a popular Cabaret Show "Passion" at the Lake Tahoe Horizon Casino Resort on the South shore in Stateline, Nevada. It was New Year's weekend, and I was the Vice President of Marketing for the resort. Gladys Knight was performing in the main showroom, The Grand Lake Theatre. A storm was coming through the Sierra's, and it looked like no one was going to be coming or going for a few days. The Cabaret show was packed so I went in to go on stage prior to the show to invite those attendees to come to the Gladys Knight show at a special price. I had a tuxedo on. I must point out here that the Cabaret Show was an adults only show, that adds to the story for sure. As I went backstage, Kenny was sitting on a cocktail table reading the local showbiz newspaper. Several of the dancers were milling about, in various stages of dress. By then, three burly stagehands made their way rushing towards me, an intruder. Kenny looked over at me and asked, "Hotel casino executive?" I replied yes, he waved off the stagehands and I went about my business. I did that before each Cabaret show and it worked quite well for the main showroom attendance. A week later, I drove into the parking lot and got out of my car. Just ahead was Kenny and his close friend, mentor and sponsor, Paul Krasny, a famous Hollywood Director. Kenny had finished his run with the show and was getting ready to drive back to home to Southern California. I stopped and told him that I had seen the full show and complimented him on his performance. I also told him I had some ideas for future projects and would be in touch. Getting in the car, Kenny turned to Paul and said, "Right, like that's ever going to happen." Being the ultimate sponsor, Paul said, "And how do you know that?" Two weeks later I called Kenny about headlining a large regional World Chili Cookoff concert in the main showroom. We had an awesome conversation and instantly became friends. The only downside to the story, from Kenny's perspective, was having to call Paul and tell him he had been "right, again." Until he passed on September 5, 2016, after headlining a comedy show in Laughlin, Nevada, Kenny, and I did hundreds of projects together. More importantly though, we were pals. We golfed together at Bandon Dunes in Oregon, went on the Catalina Express to visit his lifeguard stomping grounds in Avalon on Catalina Island, co-produced Comedy shows series in California, Oregon, Nevada, New Mexico and so much more. One of our favorite things was having dinner together. We also had several "Pink Panther" movie marathons at his place in North Hollywood. One of the highlights and most memorable moments of our longtime friendship was at my 2015 Roast/Toast of 30 years in gaming and 65th birthday dinner party/ concert in Las Vegas at Primm Valley Casino Resorts. Kenny did a wonderful performance as usual, but then did something out of the ordinary and closed his part of the show singing Mickey Newbury's song Old Friends, "that's all that matters in the end." It was way beyond special for me. The roast is still on YouTube: Don Kennedy Roast Primm 2015.

One of our favorite memories was at an Orange County Country Club where we played golf in a celebrity charity event (he was known as the Golf Comic due to hundreds of appearances in tour-naments). We were with one of our favorite NFL players, Raider/ Broncos, and USC Captain Rod Sherman. My shot landed in the rough surrounding a large sand trap near the green. I carefully positioned myself on the edge to make my next shot. I lost my balance (imagine that) and fell into the trap. Kenny held out his putter and tried to pull me out but alas, I lost grip and fell back into the trap on the back. I decided to make the best use of the situation and made a sand angel. Rod pretended not to be with us as another foursome arrived. I did rake the trap, I might add. Ah, Donny and Kenny at their very best!

Kenny was an amazing, talented, and versatile performer, but his great contribution to our world was that of a sponsor to countless souls seeking recovery. I cannot count high enough to tell the number of times he answered his cellphone and excused himself because, "I have to take this Donny, someone's in crisis." Of course, I always understood. So many folks owe their recovery in part to Kenny. Many became lifelong close friends.

Kenny's family includes son Mike Davis, grandson Christopher Davis, sister Pam Bouillon, wife Deborah Dean Davis and wife Patti Phoenix plus nieces and nephews. His other family is his beloved AA family.

Kenny Davis, as Inspector Clouseau would say, "until the case is solved!" Good Day!

Jackie Brett was born and raised in Chicago, Illinois, and I in the Milwaukee area of Wisconsin. Fate would have it that we would both move to Las Vegas, Nevada in the late 1970's and both be in the journalism/entertainment/tourism arena at the same time. Lifetime, close friends does not even begin to describe our wonderful relationship over these many decades. Her many life credits include Hollywood model and actress, journalist/columnist, author, tourism executive, race promotor, judge for the prestigious Romero Casino Marketing Awards, volunteer for the Walker Furniture annual holiday program, speaker/lecturer, publicist for numerous organizations, Advertising/Entertainment/Marketing Director for Casino Resorts and so much more. Oh, and mom for countless wonderful dogs over the years. She is married to longtime partner and Las Vegas media executive Mel Carter. I am so very proud to call both of them two of my best friends.

One of Jackie's amazing talents is being the unofficial organizer of all of her countless friends. Every Tuesday is dinner and a movie night at a local pub and movie theater. Every Friday is Happy Hour at a local restaurant. She is the glue to holds it all together. She also has become a master mover of friends. Most of us dread that text or phone call asking us to help move family or friends. Jackie embraces it. She finds it to be a wonderful time to catch up.

Jackie's career has been amazing especially because it is so varied. She wrote the book "Fabulous Las Vegas," available on Amazon and elsewhere. It is an awesome photo book in collaboration with famed Vegas photographer Larry Hanna. She writes the popular and informative Brett's Vegas View which has been featured all over the West Coast in newspapers in Denver, San Jose, Los Angeles, Las Vegas, Phoenix, San Diego, Long Beach, Orange County, Albuquerque, Dallas and many more. Her writing is so well known that the University of Nevada Las Vegas has a collection of it from 1977 to 1996 in its Special Collections department. As a key staff member for the Nevada Commission on Tourism, she opened the Las Vegas office, oversaw Motorcoach marketing, Motorsports Marketing, and rural Nevada tourism efforts. A sought-after speaker, Jackie also taught Special Events for the Clark County/Southern Nevada College. She has received several prestigious awards including the Professional Women's Achievement Award from the Las Vegas Chamber of Commerce.

She served as a key Marketing Executive for Las Vegas Casino Resorts like the Sahara, Imperial Palace, Circus Circus, Silverbird, Silver City and Harrah's.

Jackie and I could tell stories about each other for hours and hours and hours. We have shared so much over the years including my enjoyment of being a guest at her home for major holidays. I have even been Santa Claus one year for her guests (and the dogs, of course) at Christmas. I will share that one story here.

As I mentioned, Jackie invited me to Thanksgiving and Christmas dinner every year when I lived in Las Vegas. Being in the Casino hospitality business, I rarely could attend. One year I realized I could leave work a bit early and be able to join in at dessert time. There were a few dozen close friends of Jackie and Mel at the dinner party. I texted Jackie and told her I was able to break away and join in after the hour drive. Plus, I told her I would come dressed as Santa. She was thrilled with both messages and kept the Santa secret. She knew it would be a fun surprise for all gathered. I headed out and drove to their home with my trusty Santa suit duffle bag. About two blocks from my destination, I realized that I did not have a plan for changing into the suit. I could not do it at their home as every room was filled. Time for Plan B. Fortunately it was now dark out. About a block away from their home I noticed that on one side of the street was an apartment complex with a high wall facing the street. On the other side of the street was another high concrete wall facing the street with homes behind it. So, I pulled up at the curb next to the wall near the houses. I had a large SUV at the time, so I opened both the passenger's door and back door creating a somewhat protected changing space. So far, so good. Normally it takes between 20 and 30 minutes to "suit up" as us Santa's call it. Now half-dressed and half undressed, I got that panicked feeling when I fully realized what this all must have looked like. What if someone in the apartment complex across the street peered out their window, what if someone walking their dog on the sidewalk passed between me and the wall, what if a vehicle came down the road and their headlights caught of glimpse of my change-out? What if it were a patrol car? Adding to the panic, I was struggling pulling on my two big black boots without anything to steady myself with. Sure enough, I lost my balance and fell backwards full force banging the back of my heart on the concrete sidewalk. Laying there half dressed, I could only wonder what this would look like if I passed out. Those who know me well know that I can be a "tad" accident prone, so none of this should come as a surprise! GOOD GRIEF!!! I am sure it is because of that special Christmas magic, but I was able to pull myself back together, finish changing and make my way to the home of my hosts. I made the grand Santa entrance, took all kinds of photos, and toasted everyone. I was even able to take some fun photos with Jackie and Mel's dogs. I finally went into the bathroom and was able to change out before anyone figured out what was going on. Whew! I was able to make a second entrance as just little old me and no one knew except for Jackie. Even Mel did not figure it out. Mission accomplished, kind of.

Jackie Brett is that special kind of lifelong friend that everyone should be truly lucky and fortunate enough to have.

John Sydney (Quiroga) Romero, acclaimed pioneer Casino Marketing Guru, inventor of the Blackjack Tournament, author of four books, renowned magazine column writer, mentor to countless casino executives, Casino consultant, namesake of the International Romero Awards for Casino Marketing excellence, Casino Hotel Marketing Executive, much sought after guest speaker/lecturer… have I left anything out? Oh, yes, LEGEND! If it happened in the wonderful world of Casino Marketing, John left his imprint on it for sure. He received the 2004 Lifetime Achievement Award for Casino Marketing plus several prestigious Echo Awards from the Direct Marketing Association of New York.

I had the unique opportunity to work with John several days a week for two years at the Lady Luck Casino Resort in downtown Las Vegas in the late 1980's. He invited me to be on the esteemed judge's panel for the International Casino Marketing Awards, named after him, The Romero's. Each year our wonderful, eclectic panel of Jackie Brett, Jack Breslin, Toby O'Brien, Amy Fantor, Dennis Conrad, Christine Faria, and others would meet for several days and judge the hundreds of entries. It was the highlight of the year for us. So many stories to tell about those judging events, so little time.

It would take all of the pages of this book just to recap John's life and career. His family includes wife Robin and son Troy, wife Michelle and grandchildren Kylie and Lucas. Son Joshua and grandchildren Chris, Mike and Dan. Son Dana and granddaughter Sydney. John passed on April 30, 2015. I missed the opportunity of him "roasting" me at an event in my honor later that year. He would have had a field day. John actually gave me my nick name, "The Phantom," which I will explain in a bit.

John's career was a fascinating one, his family was in the vaudeville business. He was raised by his grandparents in Ft. Worth Texas and lived in Southern California. He graduated from San Jose State. He was a well-known Sports Editor for the daily Las Vegas Review Journal, TV Sportscaster, and media personality. He also worked as a boxing judge for professional fights in Nevada. His career really took off as Director of Marketing for the famed Sahara Casino Hotel where he worked for two decades. That led to the founding of the International Gaming Promotions company. The entire gaming tournament concept was born. In 1980, John formed his own consulting company and enjoyed great success. He wrote two highly acclaimed casino books, "Casino Marketing" and "Secrets of Casino Marketing." He also wrote two other books, "Las Vegas The Untold Stories" and a 2013 novel, "The Eisenhower Enigma."

Two stories I must share about John and me. My casino career has taken me all over the country, I have lived and worked in thirteen cities in seven states while Marketing for Casino Hotels and Resorts. Since I worked in these properties long before personal computers and contact apps, John kept track of me on his black book address book, a spiral notebook. He had to use liquid white out on almost a dozen addresses as I moved around. Finally, John ran out of spaces on the "K" page because of me. He sent me a bill for a replacement address book and said, "I'm going to start calling you The Phantom because I have such trouble finding you." It stuck.

The second story happened at Lady Luck Casino Resort where I served as the Marketing Director. The property was doubling in size, and it was a very busy time. John was a key consultant at the property, and we worked together for two years. It was a highlight of my career. I learned more in two years than in all of life. Being in the late 1980's, computers were not the typical way of communication. There were lots and lots of paper files back then. Everything was printed out. I was known to save everything just in case I "needed" it for something. So, my desk and my credenza were piled high with papers. In my defense, each pile was in order by category: entertainment, direct marketing, advertising, publicity, special events, etc. The "clutter" drove John nuts. Several times he inquired why I had all of it. One Monday I came into the office and every single piece of paper was gone both from the desk and the credenza. I actually looked to see if my nameplate was still on the door or if I had lost my job. It was a mystery for several days until John came back for the week. He acts surprised, but finally fessed up. He had put all of the papers in neat piles in a vacant office near mine. He laughed as he asked if I had actually missed or needed anything in the piles! Point made.

John Romero, truly the man, the myth, and the LEGEND!

Mualeava Lene has managed every major showroom and night-club in Waikiki, Hawaii as well as Southern California and Las Vegas clubs. I met him a decade ago through his cousin Runi Tafeaga, producer of the famed Hot Lava Polynesian Revue. I had hired Runi's show numerous times over the years, and we had become good friends as well. Runi introduced me to Lene (he goes by his last name as it is easier for everyone) and our friendship has grown especially when I moved to Hawaii. I am not sure if there is anyone in the entire Hawaiian island chain as well as his homeland of Samoa that he does not know. I can also say he has never met someone whom he does not call friend.

Waikiki and Honolulu have known some amazing entertainers over the years and Lene has worked with them all. The legendary Don Ho, Hoku (Don's daughter), Al Harrington, ZuLu, The Society of Seven, The Magic of Polynesia show, Elvis in Hawaii, Cirque Polynesia Hawaii, The Super American Circus, the Follies of Polynesia, Tihati's Polynesian show, Kimo Kahohano, Danny Kaleikini, plus countless island single performers and duos. He was also involved in many TV shows and movies filmed in the islands.

Lene really knows how the celebrate special occasions. There are no birthdays in his world, it is birthday months, and you celebrate the whole month long! It seems like every Saturday night the entire year is someone's birthday. Lene regularly holds court at the legendary Waikiki eatery The Chart House, owned by close friends Yana and Joey Cabell. Joey is a surfing and waterman legend in the islands and wife Yana is surely the first lady of Kahala. They are the best of the best. The wonderful marina view restaurant was opened in 1968 and lasted through a fire and the pandemic. It is a true Waikiki treasure. Lene counts among his good friends the owners and staff of many Waikiki restaurants he connected with during his long and amazing career. The Waikiki and Honolulu hospitality industry is a close knit Ohana. Everyone knows and takes care of each other.

Lene has a wonderful, impish, creative sense of humor. He is also well known for "tasting" your drinks and desserts. Never look away for too long or both will surely vanish! One of his other favorite tricks is to tell restaurant servers that someone at his table is celebrating a birthday so that a complimentary dessert is served. His bag of tricks is bottomless!

Two fun stories about Lene and I. Lene has a deep voice and thick Samoan accent. If you are with him all the time, you do not notice it as much. However, when you only talk with him a few times a year as I did before moving to Hawaii, it can be a challenge to totally understand each word. Years ago, when I was visiting the islands, I brought my special friend Dawn Bredimus of Lincoln City, Oregon. We were to join Lene at a local restaurant for pupu's (appetizers) and drinks. We arrived at the Chowder House restaurant at the harbor only to find it closed. I called Lene and told him we had arrived, he said he did not see us at the entrance. This went on for a few minutes until Dawn got on the cellphone with Lene and understood him much better that we were to be at the Chart House! Now, of course, I know of Lene's close friendship with the owners of that famous restaurant, but at the time I thought I had the right location. Embarrassing to say the least, but still a fun story.

The second story is about Father's Day 2020. Lene had invited me to celebrate with his entire family at the home of his nephew Amosa F. Amosa in Ewa Beach. I was so honored and happy to be asked to join in. Unfortunately, I got lost (imagine that) and turned the wrong way on the final street to get to their home. I finally made it, about 15/20 minutes late. When I arrived, I apologized to all of those gathered. Amosa had a very serious look on this face and said I would have to do a Samoan song and dance for arriving late. He finally smiled and said, "Anyone who is a friend of Lene's is a friend of ours," and we began the event. I was going to tell everyone they were truly about to see that "white men can't dance," but I escaped my punishment! It was a wonderful, memorable event with more fresh seafood than I have ever enjoyed, plus my first taste of fu'alifu ulu (breadfruit with coconut milk). I shared a table with an amazing couple,

Pastors Tuli and Ariella Sai Amosa. The fellowship with all of the several dozen "Aiga" (family) attending was truly special. I will always remember the day.

Lene's immediate family (Aiga) includes son Jared and granddaughter Madison, "Maddie." His mother was Vitolia and father Olo. Brothers are Usala, Tulilele and Mualeava. Sisters are Fetalai Amosa, Fesilafa'i Veavea, Matapa and Tua Lene Sila. Plus, lots and lots of nieces, nephews, cousins and more.

Mualeava Lene, truly one of a kind, one of the absolute best people on our planet. If you are among those fortunate enough to know him, you already know what I mean. Love you, Lene!

Gilbert Francis Lani Damian Kauhi or "ZuLu" or "Z," was also one of a kind. A talented actor, singer, entertainer, beachboy, family man, Hawaiian language, and culture preservation activist, and so much more. A true island icon. He was from Hilo on the big island of Hawaii. He performed in countless big production shows on all of the major showroom stages in Waikiki and Honolulu for decades. I met "Z" in the mid 1980's when he was headlining a production show on the American Hawaii Cruises SS Constitution, a classic ship. Its sister ship was the SS Independence. We ended up meeting every night after his performance in the back of the ship for pu pu's (appetizers) and drinks, often toasting with cognac. It was like we had known each other for decades. When I left the ship, we exchanged contact information and stayed in touch.

When I moved to Lake Tahoe to market a Casino Resort there on the South shore, I invited "Z" to headline numerous Polynesian style Luau productions featuring my friend Runi Tafeaga's renowned HOT LAVA show. The events packed the 1, 300 seat Grand Lake Theatre where Elvis Presley had performed. We even added an Elvis look-alike several times to sing "Blue Hawaii." "Z" had starred in the original Hawaii Five-0 hit TV show portraying Detective Kona Kalakaua. He also appeared on numerous TV shows. He introduced me to his good friend Herman Wedemeyer who portrayed Sergeant/Detective Duke Lukela on the TV show. Herman also became a longtime good friend and joined us for several of the Luau shows. A dedication to him follows this one. One of my favorite ZuLu stories involves the Lake Tahoe performances. "Z" was a very serious entertainer. He rehearsed and rehearsed. Each show was special to him. Runi acted as MC for the shows and was, and still is, more loose, casual, and spontaneous. He likes to have fun and mix things up. He was the perfect guy to plan a really fun on-stage prank on ZuLu. There was a wonderful plump size comedienne in Lake Tahoe, Joy Michelle. She was always ready for anything, so, a perfect co-conspirator! We had Joy dress up in a full Polynesian hula dancer costume complete with a very large coconut shell top. She was standing off stage as "Z" went on stage to sing the popular Hawaiian wedding song. As he crooned for all of the married couples in the packed audience, the music stopped midway through the song as Joy came out singing "I've got a lovely pair of coconuts." She sang and danced up to ZuLu, who was now standing in stunned silence, jaw dropped and totally befuddled. As she saddled up to him, she suddenly gave him a fast, hard, sideways hip hula movement and almost knocked him over. "Z" literally did not know what had hit him. As Joy finished her number, "Z" walked off the stage and downed a full glass of Cognac. Herman, Runi and I were bent over roaring in laughter as were all of the HOT LAVA band and dancers, the stagehands and audience. "Z" never did finish the song as everyone went back on stage for the finale. I do not think "Z" was ever the same. Plus, at every performance we did together in Lake Tahoe and later in Reno at the Reno Hilton, he always kept an eye out for Joy, just in case. Ah, those were the days.

I miss you "Z."

Herman Wedemeyer or "Squirmin' Herman" was from Hilo on the big island of Hawaii. Before his days as "Duke" on Hawaii

Five-0, Herman was a famous football star. Herman's brother was famed island football coach Charlie Wedemeyer, who played for Michigan State and is the subject of the 1988 movie "Quiet Victory: The Charlie Wedemeyer Story." Herman was a halfback/tailback for St. Mary's College in Moraga, Ca. He was drafted in the first round by the Los Angeles Rams and played for the AFL Los Angeles Dons and Baltimore Colts. He also played minor league baseball. Later in life Herman was elected to the Honolulu City Council and the Hawaii State Assembly. He has been inducted in the College Football Hall of Fame, Hawaii Sports Hall of Fame, Polynesian Football Hall of Fame, and St. Mary's College Football Hall of Fame. In his acting days, he also appeared on the original "Magnum P.I." and other TV shows. I truly enjoyed the many times we had to share dinner and "talk story" as it is known in the islands. Herman was a true gentleman and a wonderful person who gave back to his beloved Hawaiian Islands.

Herman Wedemeyer and Gil Kauhi, our heavenly Hawaii Five-0.

33 years and counting. That is how long I have known the Lum, Leong, Ah Yo and Kaaihue families in Hawaii. What an absolutely wonderful relationship it has been and continues to be. In the dedication to Joel Leong earlier in this dedication section of the book, I explained how we all met, so I will not repeat that. There are also some additional stories spread throughout the book about the families. I will just add some special thoughts here about the family members and that friendship that grows with each day.

When I moved to Makaha Valley on the Waianae Coast of Oahu the end of 2019, my family and friends on the mainland were concerned since I was single and would be living alone. Makaha Valley is a rural area on the far west end of the leeward side of Oahu, about an hour drive from Honolulu. I reassured all of them that I had a very special and treasured Hawaiian Ohana that would look after me. And anyone who truly knows me understands that I need a lot of looking after, to say the least!

I could write volumes about each of these wonderful folks, but I will try to keep it to some special highlights.

I call Marmionett "Marmie" Ka'aihue everyone's Auntie or Aunty. She is that special glue that holds everything together. She has been a principal key staff member of Creative Holidays, TRU, and Cruise Holidays Hawaii from its beginning. She is part of the talented Beamer musical family. I also met and became friends with her awesome niece Manono Beamer who lives on the big island of Hawaii. She attended the Hawaiian language Olelo classes with me as did Marmie. They both were witnesses to my many "interesting" attempts at mastering the language. I had the distinct pleasure in mid-December 2021 to be Santa for Marmie's great granddaughter, Punakea, also her first birthday. What an honor. No one in the family knew what she had arranged. I had changed into my Santa suit at Marmie's home, then drove around the block and arrived in my car beeping the horn. I then stepped out and did the old Ho-Ho-Ho. Stunned faces all around. It was perfect! The master planner at work as she always is. Marmie's husband, Charlie, was on the 1960 Oakland Raiders and a scout for famed San Francisco 49ers Head Coach Bill Walsh. He was also a football coach as well. Marmie is a fierce advocate for the Hawaiian heritage, culture, and language. She freely gives of her time, energy, and knowledge in all these areas. As an example, when I was Marketing Director for the businesses of the Pueblo of Acoma in New Mexico, she assisted me in connecting their Board of Education with Hawaiian immersion schools on the North Shore. It was also coordinated through the efforts of former State Senator Clayton Hee. The Acoma's were actively trying to restore and preserve their native language, Keresan. My CEO at the Acoma Business Enterprises, Marvis Aragon Jr., had joined me for a trip to Hawaii and got the ball rolling. Marvis, an Acoma, also served as First Lieutenant Governor for the Pueblo plus later on the Board of Education. It was and is an immense help in a profoundly important project for the Pueblo. A fun story about Marmie and I happened after I moved to Oahu. I started being invited to the same family events that Marmie would typically attend, and I would playfully call her my date. We had always poked fun at each other back and forth for decades. One of the family friends actually thought that we were a couple. Several times she would ask Marmie if I were coming to a particular gathering and Marmie would reply, "I don't know," or "I don't know where Don is." Finally, the family friend asked in exasperation how a couple could not know where each other were. It was perfect! They did set her straight and she roared in laughter. I absolutely love spending time with Marmie, we share many things including a complete lack of cooking skills. Or, as many people would say, we are both culinary challenged! I love you Marmie.

The Lum family, matriarch Florence (Flo), patriarch Kenneth (Ken), sons Stan, Barney and Preston, daughters Didi and Lissa are so special to me I cannot quite put it into words. I loved sitting with Flo and Ken on my visits to the islands. Since I moved around the country in my career, I was able to "talk story" about my latest job and the region I lived in. They both lived well into their nineties. Ken worked as a pharmacist and stayed working part-time late in life. He called working as a senior or Kupuna "mind aerobics." I always remember that. Didi, a caring, sincere, giving, lovely lady, was the public face of Creative Holidays/Travel Resources Unlimited with the slogan "Didi Ah Yo and away we go!" Her husband Paul was in charge of public relations. Paul was also a great musician. He often called me "handsome," to which I would reply, "I think you need glasses, Paul!" He had a heart of gold. Both passed way too early in life. I had the real pleasure of meeting and knowing Paul's brothers Herman and Kaipo as well as his daughter Samantha. Lissa Leong and Preston Lum now head up Creative Holidays/Cruise Holidays. Lissa is a devout Christian, who just like her sister Didi, has a heart as big and deep as the ocean. She pulls everything together at work, in church and at home. She shares her time with her two awesome and amazing boys, world traveler Kala'e, (I think he's moved around as much as I have!) a Lieutenant Colonel in the US Air Force and "Super Dad" Ryan, Hawaiian Airlines staff member and their families. I adore her. Brother Barney lives in the Los Angeles area and I shared many wonderful luau nights with him during the Pro Bowl weekends. He also has taught me so much about aviation and the skies above us just from his Facebook page. It brightens up my day to visit with him. Preston could easily be my younger brother, much, much younger! We share so many likes; golf, cigars, wine, sports, travel, beer, did I mention beer! He has an infectious laugh, a playful sense of humor and is also known for his catch phrases, "just kidding!" and "cheers, big ears!" I also enjoy knowing Preston because I get to spend time with his awesome family which includes his wife, the very lovely and creative Tammy Tinfo (yes, she is the BETTER half), talented and gorgeous daughter Mia and three amazing, accomplished, caring and true island watermen sons Eric, Chase, and Spencer. I have been fortunate to watch all of the Lum and Leong kids, and now grandkids, grow up from birth. They all make their families proud. It is an honor and a privilege to know them all. I could not ask for better Ohana to keep an eye out for me.

Several stories to share in addition to the two earlier in this book.

Every year, fifteen to be exact, I visited Hawaii for the NFL Pro Bowl with the two families. I would often bring friends and co-workers. The night before the game, we would all join in for a backyard luau with Paul's band playing and Master Chef Preston cooking. In my defense, this was pre-Siri, pre-cell phone, etc. On the way to the luau, I always missed a left turn onto Nehoa Street from Punahou Street. Also in my defense, (sounds like I need a lawyer, doesn't it?) that street sign was and still is badly faded. Instead, I would keep going straight until it was obvious that I had missed the turn. I would stop at a payphone (remember those?) and call their home. Preston would answer and yell out loudly for everyone to hear, "it's Don, he's lost!"

Paul and his two brothers were big men, Paul especially. His special beverage of choice during the luaus and stadium tailgates was a homemade celebratory plum wine. One year as he tried to sit down on a lawn/beach chair, and it collapsed under him. Herman and Kaipo remarked almost in unison, "oh Paul, what have you done" and everybody cracked up. Later Preston told me it was not the first time it had happened.

Paul visited Lake Tahoe when I was Marketing the Lake Tahoe Horizon Resort. We went out at sunset on the hotel yacht which had been Elvis Presley and Colonel Parker's favorite getaway. After sunset, we headed back to the marina. It was a crystal clear, dark night and the stars were out in all their glory. Paul laid back on one of the yacht's bench seats and teared up. I looked over concerned and asked him if everything was OK. He said, through tears, yes, I used to go night fishing with my father when I was a boy and loved laying back on the seat and watching the stars. "It all flooded back on me right now," he said. Simple pleasures in life can be so very meaningful.

Another fun story, which shows how very small the world really is, involves Preston and me. In late October 2021, Preston was to lead a group of two dozen cruisers on the Holland America Lines' Koningsdam for a 7-night California Coastal cruise. His group was a close-knit collection of family and friends. The group flew to the departure port of San Diego a few days ahead. Preston flew the day before. Problem is everyone's covid test results came back negative, but his was not posted yet. If not posted in time, he would have to get a second test taken at the departure dock. He met up with his group and guided them through the embarkation process. He is, as are his fellow travel company executives Lissa and Marmie, the ultimate group leaders/facilitators. As departure time got closer, Preston still did not have his test results. Back up four days earlier for my story. I had traveled from my home in Hawaii to my birth state of Wisconsin to attend the wedding of my nephew Keith to his lady Brianna. It was a 10-day trip which allowed for lots of family time including my brother, sister-in-law, nieces and great niece and great nephew. Four days before I was a leave, I got an urgent email invitation from Holland America Line's offering a free stateroom on, yes, you guessed it, the Koningsdam's 7-night California Coastal cruise from San Diego. The cruise line was trying to fill cabins and as a single traveler, I was a prime cruiser to invite. I took the offer, changed flights, and went for my covid test. That was another whole story in itself, so I will spare you the details! I flew into San Diego for my overnight. I went to the cruise ship dock still not having my test results. I finally went to the on-site rapid test area (which I dubbed the time-out room). I took the test and waited on a chair for the results. There were a dozen or so other people taking tests and waiting. I looked over at the check-in desk where a tanned guy in shorts waited. I thought to myself that he looked a lot like my friend Preston Lum. Just then he turned to the side, and I saw his San Francisco 49ers facemask (which I had given to him) and profile. I was totally surprised. I yelled out, "Bruddah Preston!" He looked over in shock and replied, "No way, Bruddah Don, what you doing here?" We compared notes on how it all happened. Just then my technician came over the gave me my test results which were negative. I looked up, looked over at Preston and back at the technician and replied, "Can you change this to positive, I don't know if I went to spend a whole week with him!" Preston agreed, "Same here," he said. The technician, as you can imagine, looked at both of us with a confused look, well you know... So, from Hawaii to Wisconsin to San Diego for me, Hawaii to San

Diego for Preston and we end up meeting like that. Considering the number of people onboard plus facemasks, his hosting a group, etc. we may have spent 7 days on a ship together and never seen each other. Instead, we had a wonderful, memorable cruise. It really is a small, small world after all!

One last story, also about the Pro Bowl week, was our annual golf outing usually with 25/30 golfers who had all come over from the mainland as Creative Holidays' guests. All eight golf carts were ready to head out. Unfortunately, I happened to be in the lead cart and started us out without knowing where I was going. The other carts followed thinking I knew the course well. I took us to the tee box for the 18th hole instead of the first. That was the last time I was allowed to be in the lead cart if I remember correctly. One truly funny thing happened on one of the first holes at the tee box. I was with Preston and my friend Kenny Davis. As I swung my club, at the very top of the swing, a bird flew out of a bush nearby and went right into the club, stopped in midair dazed and finally flew away. Of course, Preston tried to tell me it was a rare, protected species bird. Ah, just another day in the life of Santa Don!

Mahalo Nui Loa to my wonderful Hawaiian Ohana!

VERY SPECIAL TRIBUTES

I have made a lot of dedications in this book, but as a publisher once told me, "Never worry about sharing too many dedications, forever published in print, is forever remembered." In addition to these three, fond memories of all those who have gone before us.

MARG MCARDLE

This is for Toby O'Brien and the McArdle Ohana (family). Remembering Marg McArdle, from New York to Las Vegas to St.

George, Utah. A lover of the great outdoors, national parks, lakes, streams, oceans, mountains, and everything in between. A special fondness for the "Garden Isle" of Kauai, Hawaii. Remembered by Toby, daughter Diane, son Michael, family, and friends. Always remembered, always treasured.

TULILELE FA'ASAFUA AMOSA

This is for the Amosa, Tagovailoa and Lene "Aiga" (families). A celebration of life for Pastor Tuli, Pastor Dad, and Coach Tuli. Born in American Samoa and passed 8/8/2021. He lived in Ewa Beach, Oahu, Hawaii, was Pearl Harbor Navy Shipyard Supervisor, Pastor of The Message of Peace Ministry, "Savali Ole Filemu" church in Ewa Beach, Oahu, Hawaii. Coach for the Ewa Beach Sabers youth football program. Known and loved for his huge smile, huge heart, and giving, loving nature. Everyone he met was forever drawn to him. Remembered by his parents mother Fetalai, father Faasafua, wife Pastor Ariella Saipeti Tagovailoa-Amosa and children Tuli, Myron, Adam, Amarxus, Siua Tichael Nisa and Mana. Brothers are Tautua, Amosa, Lene, Kaisa and Allen. Sisters are Luapi, Tafailagi, Ruthgie, Matagi, Marie and Titilimulimu. I shared Father's Day 2020 dinner with Tuli, his wife and his family. The love that was at that home in Ewa Beach was so warm and true. A wonderful man dedicated to our youth, his congregation and family. A man larger than life, but humble in spirit. Godspeed Pastor Tuli.

HELEN "SUNBEAM" DESHA BEAMER

This is for Manono, Marmie, Ulu and the Beamer Ohana (family).

At "Sunbeams" resting place at Valley of the Temples in Kaneohe, Oahu, Hawaii, niece Manono showed me the many family stone plaques and said, "Don, these are for the generations to come to remember her." And so, inside the pages of this book, this is as well. Her family wrote this tribute to her.

Helen Ka'alo'ehukaiopua'ena Beamer became "Sunbeam" when her two-year old brother, Milton Ho'olulu Desha Beamer Jr. looked at a framed picture of a darling cherub hanging above her crib and exclaimed to his mother, "Look Mama, it's our little Sunbeam!" And thus began 94 years of Sunbeam in our lives. She was born December 11, 1927 in Honolulu, the second of three children of Milton Ho'olulu Desha Beamer Sr. and Mildred Ka'alo'ehukaiopua'ena Copp Beamer. Her younger brother, Edwin Mahi'ai Copp Beamer, was born one year later. All three children sang beautifully from the time they were very young. Sunbeam was gifted with a rich contralto voice. Her early-stage billing read: "The Haunting Voice of Sunbeam," she could mesmerize an audience with her beautiful voice. Much of her young life was spent in Hilo with her Grandmother Helen Desha Beamer, for whom she was named, and Grandfather Peter Carl Beamer Sr. And, of course, brothers and cousins always by her side. She was a 1945 graduate of Kamehameha Schools and served in the U.S. Marine Corps.

In 1959 brother Mahi'ai brought Sunbeam home to Honolulu from Las Vegas specifically to be on his Capitol recordings. The Remarkable Voice of Hawaii's Mahi Beamer In Authentic Island Songs and his second album, More Authentic Island Songs by Mahi... Hawaii's Most Remarkable Voice. Both albums showcased Mahi'ai, Sunbeam and their Aunt Harriett Beamer Magoon. The two albums were the compositions of Beamer music matriarch, Helen Desha Beamer, and a collection of traditional songs.

In 1960, The Nalani Kele's Polynesian Revue premiered in Las Vegas, featuring Nalani, Sunbeam's lifelong friend, Mahi'ai, Sunbeam, dancers, and musicians. It was a first-class authentic show that captivated guests for 16 years.

She formed many lasting friendships while residing in Palm Springs for many years by bringing her Hawaii to them through her enchanting voice, her embracing welcome and her enduring generosity. In 2017, for her unyielding support of the Aqua Caliente people, she was an honoree at the prestigious "Dinner in the Canyons" annual event of the Agua Caliente Band of Cahuilla Indians.

That same year, she was honored by the Hawaii Academy of Recording Arts with the Lifetime Achievement award.

Through all her worldwide experiences and travels, Sunbeam was always Sunbeam. She loved her family, her Hawaiian music and honu (turtles), poi, beer with a glass of ice, pork and beans with mayo sandwich, canned salmon with sweet pickle, NO ONION, and always a "PIP PIP" and "Cheering."

Sunbeam is survived by dear lifelong friends Princess Abigail Kinoiki Kekaulike Kawananakoa and Nalani Kele; Nieces Marlowe Duhaime, Heather Duhaime, Allison Beamer, Manono Beamer and Cousins.

I truly wish that I had known her. Farewell for now, "Sunbeam."

Coming Next Holiday Season, Volume 4

Thanks again for helping make this journey and adventure so much fun and rewarding. An idea that I received from several dozen readers leads me to this decision. For the holiday season of 2023, I will combine the first three books into one book, adding illustrations, lots of photos, more insights and anything else that comes up. The book will be larger in size and feature a hard cover. Kind of a coffee table book. I'm looking forward to pulling it all together. That will be the last of *Kids Say The Darndest Things To Santa Claus* from your grateful author. 'Till then, please take good care.